BETTER LEADER
HANDBOOK

BETTER LEADER HANDBOOK
SKILLS FOR SUCCESS

DDI Press

Published by DDI Press, c/o Development Dimensions International, World Headquarters—Pittsburgh, 1225 Washington Pike, Bridgeville, Pennsylvania 15017-2838.

Manufactured in the United States of America.

ISBN 978-0-578-48240-8

BETTER LEADER HANDBOOK

SKILLS FOR SUCCESS

Table of Contents

1 This Book Was Written for You

Being a Leader Is the Toughest Job You'll Ever Have

During the five decades that DDI has worked with millions of leaders, we've heard one common sentiment from leaders at every level from every part of the world: Leadership is much tougher than they thought it would be.

Leadership is so difficult because, fundamentally, it's a human experience. Whereas many people succeed early in their careers based on technical and professional knowledge, success as a leader is based on connecting with and motivating other people. Leaders need a special skill set. This book offers expertise in developing those skills in a simple package.

Because many leaders are busier than ever at work, development and skill building often take a backseat to more immediate issues. Without strong, appropriate skills, however, leaders can struggle to be effective in their roles, resulting in high stress and slow progress toward achieving organizational and career goals.

Whether you're experienced or new to the role, this book can help you become an exceptional leader. It will guide you to invest the right amount of time at the right moment. You'll develop skills that will enable you to succeed today, tomorrow, and into the future.

Invest Your Time Wisely Through Leadership 480

You can think about developing your leadership skills using a "Leadership 480" approach. Leadership 480 refers to the three horizons of time that matter most to leaders:

480 Minutes... Make every leadership moment count

Every workday you have 8 hours of opportunity—480 minutes—to advance your goals. Your success depends on the decisions you make and the interactions you have with others, minute by minute. Even in what appear to be simple situations, your choices have far-reaching consequences. Let's say you're coaching an employee with a performance problem. You could solve the problem yourself because it's faster or, instead, guide the person to find success on his or her own. Or, you might need to persuade business partners to implement a change. You could steamroll through the discussion or, instead, make sure your colleagues feel adequately involved and ready to follow your lead.

In your 480 minutes consider this: Are you handling these critical leadership moments in a way that will make tomorrow better than today?

480 Days... Advance key business drivers

In addition to addressing the daily challenges you face as a leader, you also need to help drive the organization toward long-term success. Often, organizations set a two-year horizon for achieving their goals, which is approximately 480 workdays. Although situations can be complex, just one leader with perhaps just one team can make a difference. For example, your organization might be focused on driving innovation, increasing efficiency, or creating alliances. These longer-term objectives might seem distant from your immediate team, or they might appear to clash with your daily priorities; however, taking a more strategic view will help you drive your organization's longer-term success.

As you go through your 480 days, consider this: Are you contributing to your organization's key business drivers?

480 Months... Prepare for your next career move

For most people, a career lasts roughly 40 years. DDI's work with leaders shows many didn't reach certain career goals when they thought they would. Some people are satisfied with their ultimate career paths but look back at career transitions as stressful times. They weren't prepared, and the challenges took a toll physically, mentally, and socially. By breaking down your 40-year career into 480 months, you can dedicate time each month to preparing yourself for your next opportunity. For example, building partnerships across the organization might be a small part of your current leadership role, but the next career opportunity might require building external partnerships. Make sure those next-level skills are part of your development plans.

During your 480 months consider this: Are you making improvements that will prepare you for what's next in your career?

DDI By Your Side

While you need to prepare yourself for leadership success today, tomorrow, and in the future, juggling everything at once is difficult. That's how this book will help. DDI's job is to be by your side as a coach, helping you gain the skills to address your most immediate leadership challenges and encouraging you as you pursue both your short- and long-term development goals. Consider this book to be your companion as you navigate all the critical moments of leadership, whether you're looking to be more effective in your day-to-day work or preparing to meet longer-term organizational or career objectives.

Develop Critical Leadership Skills

Yes, leadership might be the hardest job you'll ever have, but it also can bring meaning and fulfillment. You'll gain confidence and capability as you develop your skills, but how do you know which skills matter most? While working with leaders across the three 480 time horizons, DDI has discovered the most critical skills, or competencies, you'll need to succeed. Using these skills, you'll effectively handle daily leadership moments, achieve key business drivers, and get ready for your next career move.

1 Competencies describe what people say and do to achieve results in important job responsibilities, such as building partnerships, leading others, making decisions, and adjusting to change. Each competency comprises a set of related, observable behaviors called Key Actions. These Key Actions work together to help you effectively demonstrate the competency. Here's an example:

Competency ———

Facilitating Change

Leading others through the implementation and acceptance of improvements and change within the workplace.

Key Actions ———
the building
blocks for
success

Communicate what is changing and why—Explain the need for change and what the benefits might be; emphasize how change will affect performance expectations and individual, team, and organizational results.

Address resistance—Ask questions to uncover others' opinions and feelings about change; respond with empathy.

Involve others—Seek and use others' ideas when implementing changes to build their commitment to a successful implementation.

Provide implementation support—Clarify direction, specify next steps, and offer resources; hold others responsible for implementing change; track progress and measure the impact of changes.

Reward change—Recognize and reward team members who take actions that support change; communicate your confidence in others' ability to make successful changes.

DDI has identified the essential skills for frontline leader success based on a combination of hands-on experience and decades of job analysis research with organizations in every industry worldwide. The competencies in this book represent 15 of those essential skills.

Essential Frontline Leader Competencies	
Building Partnerships	Driving Innovation
Business Acumen	Execution
Coaching	Facilitating Change
Creating an Inclusive Environment	Guiding Team Success
Decision Making	Influencing
Delegation and Empowerment	

Support Competencies	
Foundational	Emotional Intelligence Essentials (EIE)
Personal Effectiveness	Adaptability Continuous Learning Driving for Results

Support Competencies

These competencies are unique and support your performance in other competencies. You can also develop each one individually to make yourself a stronger leader.

Emotional Intelligence Essentials (EIE)—EIE is foundational because it helps you build trusting relationships by increasing your self-awareness and your sensitivity to others' emotions. It can help your performance in most of the other competencies, especially those that involve leading others and collaborating to accomplish results. Explore EIE in Chapter 11. At the end of most competency chapters, you'll see how EIE supports that particular competency.

Personal Effectiveness Competencies—These competencies focus on individual styles or tendencies that persist over time and across situations, so they're more difficult for you to change. They require a different approach to learning. Explore them in Chapter 16. At the end of most competency chapters, you'll see how one or more of the personal effectiveness competencies support that particular competency.

1 What's Inside Each Competency Chapter

In each competency chapter you can explore:

- Self-insight questions to discover your strengths and development needs.
- The specific behaviors, or Key Actions, needed to demonstrate the competency effectively.
- A description of good performance and the value the competency brings to you and your team.
- How the competency helps you address the critical situations most leaders face.
- Common mistakes leaders make and how you can avoid them.
- Development activities to help you prepare for new opportunities, practice what you learn, and stretch your skills to the next level.

Personalize Your Development Journey

Improving in any competency is a journey, and your path depends on your time horizon. You'll have a shorter journey if you need to address an immediate situation: You'll focus on quick remedies and a few Key Actions. Journeys toward full proficiency in a competency will require more time, and you'll need a clear plan to develop all Key Actions through ongoing practice and skill application. If you're striving to advance a business driver or getting ready for your next career move, then you'll take the longer path.

Where are you going, and how long do you have to get there? For example, the first time you use this book you might be looking for help with an immediate situation or challenge. Maybe you have a meeting next week that's your only opportunity to advocate for the additional staff your team desperately needs. This book can help you prepare for the immediate challenge of influencing stakeholders. Later, you might return to the book if you've found that influencing skills are becoming more important in your role.

Perhaps you've taken on broader responsibilities or been promoted. Maybe you've received feedback (or realized on your own) that you need to improve your skills in a certain competency. This book also can help you with longer-term competency development.

Before jumping to a competency chapter, you should choose your development journey: immediate situation or longer-term development? Do you already know which competency you need to work on? Remember, what brings you here the first time might not be the reason you come back. You might even find yourself on simultaneous journeys: improving your skills to address a situation you're facing right now while also planning for longer-term improvement.

Start Your Journey: Where Are You Going?

1

Immediate Situation

Longer-term Development

You're facing a situation right now and need to know which competency will quickly prepare you for success.

You know which competency you'd like to develop and need a plan to take your skills to the next level.

1

Begin your journey by exploring the **Critical Leadership Moments Directory**.

Begin your journey by creating a **personalized development plan**.

2

Critical Leadership Moments are specific situations in which many leaders struggle, feel overwhelmed, and need more support.

They usually can be addressed by focusing on one or two competencies.

You'll build an **action plan** to strengthen the competency that aligns best with your professional goals. Your plan will include a development goal, specific learning activities, and ways to apply your new skills in your job.

3

Go to:
Chapter 2: Critical Leadership Moments Directory
Page 9

Go to:
Chapter 3: Build a Development Action Plan
Page 15

4

Go to relevant competency chapter(s)

2 Critical Leadership Moments Directory

As a leader, you face daily situations that stretch your skills—times when you struggle and need more support. This book calls them **Critical Leadership Moments.** These situations also create great opportunities to enhance your results and expand your capabilities. The **Critical Leadership Moments Directory** offers a list of these situations grouped into four **themes:**

Partner

Build relationships
to accomplish goals

Engage

Inspire and deploy
your team

Manage

Find and implement the
best business solutions

Drive

Move assertively
to achieve results

Next to each **Critical Leadership Moment** in the Directory, you'll find its definition and the two competencies most important for success. Here's an example:

Critical Leadership Moment	Definition	Competencies
Gain Stakeholders' Support	Persuade others to support an action or point of view, even if you don't have position power	 Influencing (161)  Building Partnerships (29)

 The **essential** competency (in the example Influencing) will help you the most with targeted development in that **Critical Leadership Moment.**

The **booster** competency (in the example Building Partnerships) will enhance your performance in the **Critical Leadership Moment.**

Here's how to use the **Critical Leadership Moments Directory** (pages 11–14) to personalize your development.

1. Select a **Critical Leadership Moment** from the directory that is most similar to the situation you are facing.

2. Next to the Critical Leadership Moment you selected, find the essential and booster competencies.

3. Since the essential competency is the most important for addressing Critical Leadership Moments, refer to that chapter first. Next, check the booster competency chapter to further enhance your performance in that Critical Leadership Moment.

   Each competency chapter offers you just-in-time advice to address the Critical Leadership Moments as well as quick remedies to avoid common mistakes. You'll also find development activities that require more focused long-term effort to help you build deeper capabilities.

Note: Support competencies (Emotional Intelligence Essentials and Personal Effectiveness) are not tied to Critical Leadership Moments in the Directory; however, they can further your development in the essential and booster competencies.

Critical Leadership Moments Directory

Partner
Build relationships to accomplish goals

2

Critical Leadership Moments	Definition	Competencies
Strengthen Relationships with Your Peers	Create supportive, collaborative relationships with your internal partners, such as other teams, functional areas, or departments	◎ **Building Partnerships (29)** ✚ Creating an Inclusive Environment (65)
Gain Stakeholders' Support	Persuade others to support an action or point of view, even if you don't have position power	◎ **Influencing (161)** ✚ Building Partnerships (29)
Expand Your Business Network	Seek new and unique business contacts to broaden your perspectives and find better solutions	◎ **Building Partnerships (29)** ✚ Creating an Inclusive Environment (65)
Navigate Organizational Politics	Appeal to various leaders across the organization by understanding and adjusting to their unique perspectives, goals, and motivations	◎ **Building Partnerships (29)** ✚ Influencing (161)
Build Relationships Outside Your Organization	Establish and sustain collaborative relationships with your external partners, such as vendors, alliance organizations, and industry groups	◎ **Building Partnerships (29)** ✚ Influencing (161)

Engage
Inspire and deploy your team

2

Critical Leadership Moments	Definition	Competencies
Empower Your Team	Build team commitment through meaningful work and motivational guidance	◎ **Delegation and Empowerment (89)** ➕ Coaching (53)
Coach a Person with a Performance Problem	Provide guidance to help a person improve a challenging performance issue	◎ **Coaching (53)** ➕ Influencing (161)
Encourage Experimentation and New Ideas	Create a team environment in which people have the confidence to question and improve processes and solutions	◎ **Driving Innovation (101)** ➕ Facilitating Change (137)
Challenge Your Team to Stretch Their Performance	Create a team environment that encourages your team members to strive for excellence	◎ **Guiding Team Success (149)** ➕ Coaching (53)
Help Others Accept Change	Manage the interpersonal challenges, resistance, and uncertainty that come with change initiatives	◎ **Facilitating Change (137)** ➕ Influencing (161)
Prepare Someone for an Ambitious Assignment	Help a team member or colleague succeed with a difficult task or challenging assignment	◎ **Coaching (53)** ➕ Delegation and Empowerment (89)
Establish Your Authority	Communicate your leadership agenda in a commanding and compelling manner	◎ **Influencing (161)** ➕ Guiding Team Success (149)
Be a Diversity Advocate	Build a team culture that acknowledges, respects, and celebrates people's differences	◎ **Creating an Inclusive Environment (65)** ➕ Guiding Team Success (149)

Manage

Find and implement the best business solutions

Critical Leadership Moments	Definition	Competencies
Find the Best Solution Despite Limited Information	Arrive at solid solutions to problems, even when information is incomplete	**Decision Making (77)** Driving Innovation (101)
Manage Information Overload	Sort through and evaluate a vast amount of information to enable quick decision making	**Decision Making (77)** Business Acumen (41)
Consider People's Differences as an Advantage	Make better decisions by including and recognizing others' diverse perspectives and experiences	**Creating an Inclusive Environment (65)** Decision Making (77)
Get Better Operational Results (quality, cost, efficiency)	Create processes and plans and make decisions to improve business outcomes	**Decision Making (77)** Business Acumen (41)
Manage the Risk Associated with Critical Business Decisions	Balance the risk and potential payoff when making crucial business decisions	**Business Acumen (41)** Decision Making (77)
Identify New Business Directions	Propose strategic shifts based on an understanding of what's happening in your business, industry, and market	**Business Acumen (41)** Driving Innovation (101)

Drive
Move assertively to achieve results

2

Critical Leadership Moments	Definition	Competencies
Provide Team Structure and Direction	Provide the team with the structure, role clarity, and guidance to accomplish key tasks	◎ **Guiding Team Success (149)** ➕ Execution (125)
Share More Responsibility with Your Team	Willingly and confidently delegate key responsibilities to team members	◎ **Delegation and Empowerment (89)** ➕ Guiding Team Success (149)
Hold Team Members Accountable for Delivering Results	Ensure employees are clear about their responsibilities and expectations for delivering results	◎ **Delegation and Empowerment (89)** ➕ Execution (125)
Make Change Happen	Get results and see progress despite the challenges and disruption of change	◎ **Facilitating Change (137)** ➕ Execution (125)
Focus the Team on Critical Business Priorities	Create plans and provide instructions to ensure the team is working on critical organizational goals	◎ **Execution (125)** ➕ Guiding Team Success (149)
Execute a Major Project or Business Initiative	Ensure that projects are thoroughly planned and resourced for successful, on-time completion	◎ **Execution (125)** ➕ Delegation and Empowerment (89)
Get Results from Innovation Efforts	Implement new ideas and solutions with structure and discipline, even when innovation brings uncertainty	◎ **Driving Innovation (101)** ➕ Execution (125)

3 Build a Development Action Plan

The journey to becoming an exceptional leader demands planning, effort, and commitment. You booked your passage when you began reading this book. To get the most benefit from your development time, use this chapter to create an action plan that focuses on your most important competencies.

While helping people all over the world improve their effectiveness, DDI has discovered the best way for you to develop as a leader. The process involves three stages:

1. **Assess**—Identify the right development targets (or competencies).

2. **Acquire**—Learn and practice the behavioral skills related to your target competencies.

3. **Apply**—Use your enhanced skills to improve your effectiveness on the job.

This chapter walks you through each stage to help you build your development plan.

Development Process

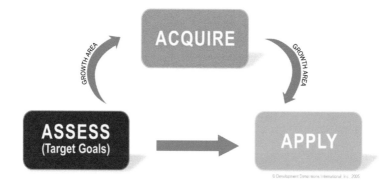

Engage Your Manager in Your Development

Your manager's commitment and support are critical as you build and carry out your plan. With the right involvement, he or she can become your greatest development advocate. Treat your development journey as a partnership.

To prepare for a discussion with your manager, think through the Assess, Acquire, and Apply sections of the Development Action Planner on the next page. You don't need to have answers to all the sections of the planner, but be prepared with some initial ideas and questions to guide your discussion as you complete the form together.

Development Action Planner

Use the **Development Action Planner** to document your plan as you build it. This form and this chapter will guide you through the **Assess, Acquire,** and **Apply** process. You can make copies and complete a form for each competency you target for development. You'll find a sample completed planner for one strength and one growth area on pages 26–27.

Strengths are competencies that you demonstrate effectively across situations. Build on your strengths to enhance your performance even further.

Growth areas are competencies that you don't demonstrate effectively and might cause you problems. Build these skills to improve your current capabilities and performance results.

Development Action Planner

Assess
☐ Strength to Leverage ☐ Growth Area

What competency will you develop (include Key Actions you will target)?

Development goal (SMART):

List the benefits to the organization, department, team, and you:

Acquire

How will you acquire the learning to achieve your goal?

Apply

How will you apply what you have learned?

How will you know you are making progress?

Development Results

Did you complete your development goal, or is more development needed?

How did you apply what you learned, and what was the outcome? What were the payoffs to the organization, department, team, and you?

Other insights from your experience?

Assess

Identify the Right Development Targets

Follow these steps to write a development goal for one competency strength and one growth area in the Assess section of the Development Action Planner:

1. Determine which competencies are most important for your career success.
2. Identify your competency strengths and growth areas.
3. Write SMART goals for one competency strength and one growth area.

STEP 1: Determine which competencies are most important for your career success.

What to think about:

This book includes 15 competencies that are important for success across most frontline leader jobs. Now, you need to decide which competencies are most important for your career success.

Consider these time horizons to help you identify the most important competencies to meet your career goals.

Your Immediate Success

The importance of a competency varies based on the responsibilities in your job. A job description gives you clues to the important competencies. Some organizations have a competency model identified for each job level. (Ask your Talent Management area.)

Are there situations in which you feel challenged or at a loss to improve results? Identifying those Critical Leadership Moments will help you identify the competencies you need to develop.

Longer-Term Success

For more strategic goals, think about which competencies will advance your organization's key business drivers. Keep in mind the organization's business plan, your boss' strategic priorities, emerging market trends, competitive threats, and changing technologies.

Career Transitions

Consider your career goals. If you're new in your job or struggling to meet performance standards, then focus on the competencies most important for your current job. But if you're performing well now and hope to take on new responsibilities or prepare for a lateral move or promotion, then focus on the competencies most important for those future jobs or roles.

○ **Engage Your Manager**

Because your manager knows which competencies have the greatest impact on job performance, identify the most important competencies together.

○ **Find Help in This Book**

The **Critical Leadership Moments Directory** in **Chapter 2** will tell you the competencies needed to address your urgent challenges. Also consider the **Support Competencies—**Emotional Intelligence Essentials and Personal Effectiveness.

Assess

STEP 2: Identify your competency strengths and growth areas.

What to think about:

Now that you've zeroed in on the most important competencies for success, you need to know which of those competencies you're good at and which you need to improve.

Seek Feedback

As you lead, people around you—your team members, peers, leaders, partners, and customers—continually watch you and evaluate your effectiveness. This makes them valuable information sources to help you understand your strengths and growth areas from a variety of perspectives. Consider insights gathered from:

- Recent performance evaluations.

- Formal and informal feedback.

- Multisource (360°) feedback surveys.

- Assessment results.

- Self-assessments.

○ **Engage Your Manager**

Ask for your manager's evaluation and specific examples to identify your strengths and growth areas.

○ **Find Help in This Book**

Use the **Self-Insight Questions** and **Common Mistakes** in each competency chapter to help you identify your strengths and growth areas. Locate ideas for gathering feedback in the **Development Activities** list.

For which competencies did you receive favorable ratings or comments? Which ones elicited negative feedback or suggestions for improvement? Look for areas of overlap where sources agree as well as places where they disagree. Does the same competency surface as a problem or a strength across situations?

Be Receptive

You might be tempted to discount others' perceptions of your strengths and development needs, especially when you disagree. Remain open-minded, listen carefully, and ask for examples to understand what you say or do to create these perceptions.

Explore Your Blind Spots

You might be surprised to learn that others think you need to improve certain skills. Blind spots are areas in which you believe you're more proficient than you actually are. They form when you lack experience or opportunities to receive feedback. Take the time to understand feedback for improvement, even if you disagree.

Discover Your Hidden Strengths

You'll often find nice surprises in the feedback you receive. Hidden strengths are competencies that you demonstrate well, without realizing the role they played in your past success. Or, you might not have had a chance to apply those skills in the past. Look for opportunities to use them to your advantage.

Assess

STEP 3: Write SMART goals for one competency strength and one growth area.

What to think about:

You've identified which competencies are important for success and which are your strengths and growth areas. Now, commit to a development goal for one competency strength and one growth area. Keep the following best practices in mind when writing development goals:

Focus on High-Payoff Goals

Balance your individual needs with the team's and the organization's needs. Which one or two competencies will have the highest payoff for your individual, team, and organization results now and in the near future?

Drill Down to the Key Actions

Instead of trying to develop an entire competency, you'll increase your chances of success if you identify one or two Key Actions that will have the most impact on your performance. By breaking down the competency into smaller components, you can focus your efforts on more targeted development activities.

Engage Your Manager

Your manager will have insights into which competencies will have the highest payoff for development.

Find Help in This Book

Review each competency's **Key Actions** to select the specific behaviors you'll target for development.

Write SMART goals

The most effective development goals are SMART:

Specific—define specific, observable results to be achieved (not tasks).

Measurable—define time frames, quantity, cost, or quality metrics to determine progress.

Attainable—are challenging, yet achievable.

Relevant—support important team or organization goals.

Time bound—specify a due date, time frame, or frequency.

Examples of SMART Development Goals

Growth Areas	Strengths
By strengthening my Delegation and Empowerment skills, I will increase my time for strategic planning by 20 percent over the next six months. **Key Action:** Identify opportunities to share responsibility.	**Because of my increasing use of Driving for Results behaviors,** my team will expedite the timeline for the ABC project, delivering to the customer five days earlier than we had committed. **Key Actions:** Establish stretch goals. Achieve goals.
By enhancing my Influencing skills, I will gain my leader's commitment to add a technical resource to our project team by the end of February. **Key Actions:** Build a compelling case. Steer commitment to action.	**I will use my strong Execution skills** to coach the ABC team leader so that team will meet the March 20 deadline. **Key Actions:** Maintain focus. Ensure accountability.

3

Acquire

Learn and Practice Behavioral Skills

Choose development activities that will help you gain or enhance your skills.

3

Everyone learns differently. For example, some people prefer to learn about new skills before practicing them. Others want to dive in and learn from experience. Consider your preferred learning style as you choose development activities that will help you learn and practice each target competency. You can use a variety of learning approaches. Usually, a combination of activities works best for skill building. Some activities are formal, such as courses, and some are less structured, such as learning from internal experts.

What to think about:

To acquire or practice skills before applying them on the job, look for learning opportunities such as:

Activities	Examples
Formal training	Classroom, web-based, and virtual courses
Leadership experts	Books, articles, blogs, podcasts, webinars, videos, and conferences
Internal or external coaches	Your leaders, peers, internal or industry experts, and professional coaches

Focus on Key Actions

You want to learn new or more effective skills and get rid of less-effective ones. This means you focus on strengthening the Key Actions in your target competencies as you avoid common mistakes. Choose development activities that target the Key Actions that you and your manager think will be most beneficial for improving your performance.

Engage Your Manager

Ask your manager to recommend formal training or internal experts to help you learn.

Practice, Practice, Practice

Acquiring leadership skills is like learning a sport. You first get fundamental instruction and then practice in a safe setting before applying new skills to more critical challenges. Choose the learning methods that work best with your current level of expertise and preferred learning environment to produce the most measurable performance improvements.

Find Help in This Book

Review the **Key Actions** and **Common Mistakes** in each competency chapter to pinpoint the behaviors to enhance and avoid. Look for **Development Activities** that allow you to learn and practice in safe situations.

Apply

Use Enhanced Skills to Boost Your Performance

For each goal, choose development activities in which you can apply your skills to work challenges. Then, determine how you will track and measure your progress.

STEP 1: Seize opportunities to use your enhanced skills on the job.

3

What to think about:

For real improvement to take place, set up purposeful opportunities to practice your new skills on the job right away. Follow these best practices:

Choose High-Payoff Development Experiences
Look for opportunities with these characteristics:

- The outcome is important to you, the team, and the organization.

- The assignment is realistic to achieve but will also increase your skill level.

- There are clear ways to measure your performance.

- You have the support of your manager, team members, and partners.

- You have access to high-quality role models, realistic practice, and feedback.

- You have the time and resources that you need to succeed.

Create Just Enough Learning Tension
Choose opportunities that create "learning tension"— that is, they put psychological pressure on you—to ensure you put forth your best effort. Challenge yourself to move outside your comfort zone. Here's a good rule of thumb: If it feels a bit scary, it probably will be a valuable development experience. Start with easier, low-risk opportunities and then ease your way into more difficult, higher-risk challenges.

Make the Most of Application Opportunities
When you commit to a development activity, prepare for it. For example, if you plan to practice new skills as you lead your next discussion, think about what you will say or do to use the Key Actions effectively. What responses do you anticipate from the people involved, and how will you address them? Share your plan for applying the skill with your manager and ask for feedback on it; be clear about the skills you're trying to improve.

○ **Engage Your Manager**

The best opportunities are often built into your current job or stretch assignments. Your manager can help you create these opportunities.

Agree on the resources and coaching you'll need; anticipate barriers to success.

○ **Find Help in This Book**

The **Development Activities** list in each chapter offers ideas for applying the competency to tasks, assignments, and special projects on and off the job.

Apply

STEP 2: Identify measures to evaluate your progress.

What to think about:

Measurement tells you when you're demonstrating a competency effectively and guides quick course correction when you're not. How will you measure the impact applying your enhanced skills had on important results? For example:

- Was your execution plan effective?

- Was the problem solved effectively?

- Did you make a good decision?

- Did you lead a productive discussion?

- Were you able to persuade people?

Engage Your Manager

Ask your manager to suggest measurement methods. Request feedback as you apply new skills to gauge your progress.

Find Help in This Book

In the Development Activities list in each chapter, you'll find ideas for gathering feedback as you apply your skills.

Examples of Measurement Methods

You have many options for measuring your application of competencies. Here are some examples:

- Short-term operating data (daily, weekly, or monthly reports)

- Longer-term operational measures (e.g., employee retention, sales, grievances, accidents)

- Annual surveys (e.g., customer satisfaction, employee engagement)

- Multisource (multirater or 360°) feedback surveys

- Completing a project within a certain time frame or budget

- Meeting quality standards

Create Feedback Opportunities

Often, the best way to measure the progress of your development is to ask people for feedback. Just as you gathered feedback to understand your strengths and growth areas in the Assess stage, you'll seek multiple perspectives from those who can observe you in action as you practice behaviors on the job. Ask for informal feedback or create a quick survey or an interview with questions that focus on the Key Actions you're targeting for improvement.

You can also ask a coach to evaluate your plan for applying a competency, observe you in meetings or discussions as you practice the skill, and then give you feedback on your strengths and areas in need of improvement.

Keep the Momentum Going

As you juggle your daily work responsibilities and your development activities, it's easy to let other commitments take priority over your development goals. To avoid this pitfall, you can use measurement to increase your accountability and make sure you turn your development plan into reality. As you focus on applying specific competencies and their Key Actions, continually ask for feedback on your effectiveness. Then, you can ask for support right away when you spot any barriers.

Using the measures you identified in the Development Action Planner, document your progress every few months in the Development Results section. Discuss your learning insights and results with your manager and your team to show that your development efforts are paying off. This will encourage you and your manager to keep going with the next phase of your development.

The development process described—Assess, Acquire, and Apply—has been tested and proven to be effective in making your leadership journey successful. But remember that you're the most powerful force in your development. The sooner you take the next step in your journey, the better.

3

Example Development Action Planner

3

Assess

☐ Strength to Leverage   ☒ Growth Area

What competency will you develop (include Key Actions you will target)?
Coaching
Key Action: Offer support

Development goal (SMART):
Increase proactive coaching so my team members are better prepared for new customer projects. Increase my coaching rating from my team from 2.5 to 3.5.

List the benefits to the organization, department, team, and you:
If people are better prepared for assignments, their confidence and results will improve. I'll need to spend less time coaching them during the project.

Acquire

How will you acquire the learning to achieve your goal?
Create a coaching plan to prepare the team for the next customer project. Ask an expert coach to evaluate my plan and give me improvement suggestions.

Apply

How will you apply what you have learned?
Prepare my team for the ZRW Security project by carrying out my coaching plan. Get their feedback after each coaching discussion and after the project ends.

How will you know you are making progress?
My team expresses confidence before the project kickoff meeting with the customer. The customer is satisfied with the team's performance. My coaching feedback and evaluation improves to at least a 3.5 average rating.

Development Results

Did you complete your development goal, or is more development needed?
Yes, I coached each team member before the project to prepare them.

How did you apply what you learned, and what was the outcome? What were the payoffs to the organization, department, team, and you?
The team expressed appreciation for the time invested in preparing them for the project. They received high customer satisfaction ratings (4.2) and my coaching rating went up to 4.0.

Other insights from your experience?
Since my team has become more confident, they are volunteering for more challenging customer projects, which they had avoided in the past.

Example Development Action Planner

Assess

☒ Strength to Leverage   ☐ Growth Area

What competency will you develop (include Key Actions you will target)?
Building Partnerships
Key Actions: 1) Seek opportunities to build relationships 2) Involve others

Development goal (SMART):
Expand my international trainer network by 50% before the March Yousoar system launch.

List the benefits to the organization, department, team, and you:
Will make the training more globally relevant and create local experts to support each region. This will ease the burden for me and other headquarters resources.

Acquire

How will you acquire the learning to achieve your goal?
Ask my current international partners to help me create a plan to expand my network. Ask them whom to involve and the best way to involve them.
Attend monthly regional meetings to understand each region's most pressing goals and training needs.

Apply

How will you apply what you have learned?
Reach out to each region to build a committed international team of system trainers. Use their ideas to tailor the training to each region's needs.

How will you know you are making progress?
Network has expanded 50%. Our group is devoting 30% less time to international training support. The training evaluation average rating has improved.

Development Results

Did you complete your development goal, or is more development needed?
Increased international involvement by 30%. The training satisfaction average rating increased from 3.2 to 4.0. Keep working on Building Partnerships skills.

How did you apply what you learned, and what was the outcome? What were the payoffs to the organization, department, team, and you?
I used the insights I gathered from my current network to expand my training team. Their ideas improved the training by making it fit each region's needs better. We're spending 20% less time in our group supporting the XYZ system.

Other insights from your experience?
Next, I want to focus on the Influencing competency. I want to be more persuasive to increase involvement further.

4 Building Partnerships

Developing and leveraging relationships within and across work groups to advance mutual goals.

The Spirit of This Competency

This competency is about creating and maintaining relationships, both within and outside your organization. Building partnerships helps you to forge alliances and accomplish goals that you couldn't accomplish alone. These relationships are the "glue" that holds together separate organizational functions (such as sales, production, and distribution) and the deterrent to dysfunctional silos that stifle efficiency. Developing relationships with vendors and partners outside your organization helps each party to expand capabilities and pursue innovative business opportunities. Leaders with strong partnership skills are seen as integrators and facilitators—they focus on collaborating, communicating openly, and ensuring that all parties work together to achieve win-win results.

Self-Insight Questions

How are you doing at Building Partnerships right now? Ask yourself:

- How often do I initiate and build new relationships within and across work groups?

- What steps do I take to learn more about my business partners' values, priorities, and goals? Do I openly share mine?

- How well do I respond to and integrate others' ideas?

- When I work with other teams or groups, how do I make sure responsibilities are clear and all parties are committed to doing their part?

- What do I say or do to make my business partners feel valued, appreciated, and included in discussions?

- How effectively do I offer information, resources, and help so that others can be more effective?

Key Actions: Building Blocks for Success

Key Actions are behaviors that work together to help you demonstrate this competency effectively.

Seek opportunities to build relationships—Look for ways to build relationships with those who have the knowledge, experience, resources, or influence to advance your work goals.

Clarify shared goals—Exchange information to determine goals and outcomes that will benefit both you and your partners. Identify issues and concerns. Summarize to check that all parties have a common understanding.

Develop others' and own ideas—Contribute your own ideas and expand on others' ideas.

Facilitate agreement—Gain your partners' commitment to ideas or actions. Use sound rationale to explain the value of actions. Confirm next steps (who will do what by when), needed resources and support, and how to track progress.

Support partners—Offer valuable information, resources, and time to accomplish win-win outcomes. Place higher priority on the group's goals than on your own.

Involve others—Ask others for their opinions and ideas.

Maintain and enhance self-esteem—Show others you value them by acknowledging their specific contributions, successes, and skills.

When you're building partnerships effectively, you'll notice:

You and your partners share a common purpose.

- There's give-and-take. Both you and your partners flex your goals to better align with each other's goals.
- Other departments or teams are more likely to disclose their intentions and strategies. They see the value you can add to their area and ask for your input and reactions.
- You're knowledgeable about other leaders and groups. You know what they're working on and how and when they can be of value to you.
- Your partners feel joint ownership of your agenda and understand how you can help one another. They're comfortable sharing concerns and offering improvement ideas.

4

You have relationships that advance important work goals.

- You're gaining synergies. Through partnerships you accomplish more together than you would have alone.
- Your partnerships tend to be mutually beneficial rather than one-sided relationships.
- You can more readily anticipate and avoid barriers in your partnerships. You have an increased awareness of the impact of your decisions and actions on your partners.
- You are a strong role model for building and nurturing relationships. You've created a work culture in which your team members also value partnerships and collaboration.

It's easy to find and attract new partners.

- You initiate new partnership opportunities, and others readily accept your invitations.
- You effectively communicate your individual, team, or organizational values and intentions to potential partners.
- You've built a network of partners and maintained those relationships over time. Your partners promote your working relationship, and they seek opportunities to work with you and your team.

Critical Leadership Moments

As a leader, you face situations, or **Critical Leadership Moments,** that stretch your skills. Building Partnerships can help you to:

Partner

▶ Strengthen Relationships with Your Peers

▶ Expand Your Business Network

▶ Navigate Organizational Politics

▶ Build Relationships Outside Your Organization

▶ Gain Stakeholders' Support

4

Building Partnerships is **essential** for success if you want to:

Strengthen Relationships with Your Peers

To create supportive, collaborative relationships with your internal partners, such as other teams, functional areas, or departments, focus on these **Key Actions:**

- **Seek opportunities to build relationships** and interact more often with people from different functional areas (e.g., sales, finance) or locations.

- **Clarify shared goals** to find out what you and your peers have in common. Ask questions to uncover—then remove—any barriers.

- **Involve others** by asking for their opinions and ideas. Try to see things from a new and more objective angle.

Also see the **Creating an Inclusive Environment** competency to be even better prepared for this Critical Leadership Moment.

Expand Your Business Network

To seek new and unique business contacts to broaden your perspectives and find better solutions, focus on these **Key Actions:**

- **Seek opportunities to build relationships** with people who can expose you to new concepts and experiences.

- **Support partners** by offering valuable information, resources, and your time. Give your network proper attention; sometimes, this means making someone else's need a higher priority than your own.

- **Involve others** by asking for their opinions and ideas. New perspectives can lead you to better, more creative solutions.

Also see **Creating an Inclusive Environment** competency to be even better prepared for this Critical Leadership Moment.

Navigate Organizational Politics

To appeal to various leaders across the organization by understanding and adjusting to their unique perspectives, goals, and motivations, focus on these **Key Actions:**

- **Seek opportunities to build relationships** and create allies across the organization. Ask: Where do decisions get made, and by whom? Identify those with formal and informal authority and find out which coalitions exist.

- **Clarify shared goals** so that your partnership is founded on mutual understanding. Explore what others are trying to accomplish; understand what they have at stake.

- **Facilitate agreement** by showing your partners what they have to gain from the proposed solution. Get firm commitment to solutions and next steps.

Also see the **Influencing** competency to be even better prepared for this Critical Leadership Moment.

4

Build Relationships Outside Your Organization

To establish and sustain collaborative relationships with your external partners, such as vendors, alliance organizations, and industry groups, focus on these **Key Actions:**

- **Clarify shared goals** and concerns. Partners might have priorities and processes that conflict with yours, so ask questions to identify concerns and to establish what you have in common.

- **Facilitate agreement** by showing your partners what they will gain by working together. Get commitment to solutions and next steps.

- **Support partners** by striving for win-win solutions, rather than what works best for you. Offer your partners information, resources, and your time.

Also see the **Influencing** competency to be even better prepared for this Critical Leadership Moment.

 Building Partnerships will **boost** your success if you want to:

Gain Stakeholders' Support

While **Influencing** is critical for persuading others and gaining their support (even when you lack position power), you'll be more influential if you've already built strong partnerships with those stakeholders. You can use your understanding of what's important to them to appeal to their needs in the most compelling way.

Common Mistakes

You can avoid common Building Partnerships errors by paying attention to how people react to your efforts.

Under Actions

When you don't demonstrate the Key Actions for Building Partnerships effectively, the results can be disappointing.

4

If you notice that:	You might be:	Try these quick remedies:
Your team works in isolation	**Missing partnership opportunities**	• Use social media to identify potential external partners but do more than "follow" them. Internally, get ideas from an organization chart or extend relationships from short-term projects. • Whom would you never dream of reaching out to? Give it a try. Look for influencers and thought leaders in your market and industry.
Partnerships quickly fizzle out	**Abandoning them at the first sign of trouble**	• Would you rather end a partnership than spend time, energy, and resources fixing it? Don't give up too quickly. Business relationships often face setbacks, such as changing priorities or limited time. Help the partnership survive these shifts.

Partners pull back or withdraw	**All take and no give**	• Make sure your partner feels valued and:
		  – Informed. Hoarding information impedes progress and damages trust.
		  – Understood. Ask about your partner's experiences, needs, and expectations.
		  – Involved. Ask for—rather than dictate—solutions.
		  – Supported. Work toward reciprocity. Offer your time and resources to help a partner achieve his or her goals.

Your partnerships are not generating tangible results	**Making assumptions about shared goals, agreement, or progress**	• Ask what others want (personal and practical needs) from the partnership. Don't assume their needs match yours. • Avoid forcing solutions. Engage passive partners. Ask for their ideas and agreement. • Define roles and responsibilities. As the partnership evolves, monitor progress. Are you getting results? Adjust anything that's not working.

Over Actions

When you demonstrate certain Building Partnerships Key Actions at an extreme level, it can lead to poor results.

If you notice that:	You might be:	Try these quick remedies:
You're overwhelmed by too many partnerships	Seeking (or staying in) the wrong opportunities	• Partnerships require a commitment of time and energy, so focus on the quality, not the quantity. Identify any that are unproductive or dysfunctional and find out why. If the partnership doesn't have sustainable value, cut ties. • Establish partnerships based on business objectives, not on personal relationships or a person's likeability. Define your goals early and specifically (e.g., What do you hope to accomplish?).
Differences between you and your partners seem insurmountable	Too focused on problems and differences	• Focus on what unites you and your partners, rather than what divides you. If opinions or agendas diverge or clash, refocus on shared goals and the benefits the partnership can bring to each of you.

Your partners seem annoyed or overwhelmed	Inundating your partners with expectations	• New partnerships can be exciting but don't overdo it:
		  – Over-sharing information can make it difficult for your partners to know what's important and what's not.
		  – Over-involving can make problem solving less productive.
		  – Over-monitoring can be alienating.
		  – Relax your approach if you're overwhelming your partners.

Your partners reluctantly agree	Focused more on problem solving than collaboration	• Your partners are not there to be "sold" on your ideas. Don't promote your ideas prematurely or too passionately. Pause frequently to ask questions, get reactions, and uncover resistance. Invite ideas. Solutions pushed aggressively have a greater chance of failure than those achieved collaboratively.

4

Development Activities

Some of these activities will help you quickly address Critical Leadership Moments. Others require a greater investment of time and resources and can be part of your longer-term development plan. Choose the activities that work best for your goals.

▶▷▷ Prepare for It... Prepare for opportunities to build partnerships.

Find the right partners—Consider your short- and long-term business goals and make a list of areas that could advance via a partnership. Reach out to those who might help you achieve your work goals. Expand your thinking about who could be a partner and connect with people from diverse areas of expertise, demographics, generations, functions, and levels. Look inside and outside your organization:

- Internally: Is there an area, team, or department your group should work with closely? Initiate a discussion with their key players. Ask your leader to recommend relationships you could build that would help the organization reach some of its goals.

- Externally: Try to initiate meetings or conversations with colleagues. Social media can help establish connections, but also meet in person at industry conferences and networking events. Consider customers and vendors as partners too. If possible, tour their facilities and get to know their business and how they conduct it.

Identify potential obstacles—Synergistic connections between groups that are very different from one another depend on overcoming substantial barriers, such as competing priorities, conflicting goals, diverse perspectives, geographic distances, and low trust. How are you, your team, and your department viewed? Are you a barrier? Do you need to overcome stereotypes? Are your differences with your partners philosophical or practical? Explore philosophical differences by learning more about one another. Adjust or remove practical challenges, such as policies or processes that others see as barriers, if they make you or your team a less attractive partner. For example, is there technology or software that would make you more accessible or improve communication? Is there a way to make a policy less restrictive, increasing opportunities for collaboration?

Prepare an influence strategy—Prepare for your next conversation with a potential partner as if it were a sales call. Why should the partner invest in the relationship? Create a business case to illustrate mutual benefits and return on investment. What would each of you contribute, and what specific tangible benefits would each of you see if you worked together? Put yourself in the partner's shoes and ask, "What's in it for me?" Anticipate possible objections and be prepared to address them.

 **Try It...** Practice building partnerships.

Set expectations early—To avoid disappointment, talk up front about expectations for the relationship. What are the short- and long-term goals? Never make assumptions; get your partners' agreement. Regularly check for changes in expectations and circumstances. At every check-in ask, "Has anything changed on your end?" Decide together when and how you should check expectations.

Remember to reciprocate—Offer to help others accomplish their goals, and they'll be more willing to help you. For new partners, focus on achieving their goals rather than yours. Although you're likely pressed for time and resources, consider ending every partner interaction with "Is there anything else I can help you with?" Ask your leader to clarify your flexibility and limits around cost and time as you build partnerships. Are your team members interested helping another team as a way to cross-train? Don't hesitate to ask your partners for help—they'll appreciate opportunities to contribute to shared goals.

Share information—When you come across information your partners would appreciate, share it, taking care not to inundate your partners. Instead, curate the information and prioritize it so you're sharing only what's timely and relevant. Holding back information or sharing it too late can erode trust. You might judiciously copy your partners on communications letting them know you're keeping them in the loop. Before you share, ask yourself, "How is this information adding value for my partner?" Also, share opportunities—events, presentations, or projects that might interest your partners. Look for ways to incorporate your partners' interests, even if you aren't directly involved in the activities.

Stay accountable to your partners—Your partners are key stakeholders, so you have a responsibility for frequent, honest, and productive communications. Check in regularly and reiterate the partners' value, even if you're in a lull or overwhelmed by other work demands. If you inadvertently make it a lesser priority, apologize for lack of effort or misunderstanding. If missteps occur, accept your share of the responsibility and don't place blame or hold grudges. Instead, recover quickly by focusing on solutions.

Acknowledge and recognize your partners—People need to be reminded of their value, and to know their time and effort are appreciated. Congratulate your partners on their accomplishments, even those outside the partnership. Watch for news and updates that mention your partners' professional contributions and acknowledge what you find. Simple comments, such as "nice work!" or "excellent results!" can build trust with your partners. Send thank-you messages when a partner has helped you and copy the person's leader.

Create a partnership-oriented team culture—Set an example for your team for building partnerships. Share the progress and outcomes of your partnerships and encourage team members to strike up their own. Be clear about when they should compete with your business partners (rarely) and when they should collaborate (frequently). Make sure your team's culture and performance metrics don't encourage competitive or selfish behavior. Find ways to acknowledge and reward team players.

4

▶▶▶ Stretch It... Apply your partnership-building skills in more challenging ways.

Reflect on your partnerships and interactions—Look back on the last few months or even the year. Make a list of your partners, including the key contact, date, brief description of the problem/opportunity, and how you handled it.

- Fill in the blanks: "Partnerships with people from [this group/department/ demographic] almost always lead to [what outcome?]" Look for trends. Are some partnerships more rewarding than others? What root causes could you address that might lead to more fruitful partnerships in the future? Are you over-generalizing and avoiding certain groups or topics because of past experience?

- Periodically review your partnerships and look for patterns. What are the circumstances when partnerships struggle versus thrive? Analyze both categories and identify what works well and what barriers exist. Are you using the same approach with every partner? Are your solutions routine, and therefore don't satisfy each party's needs? Get feedback and suggestions, perhaps from your leader, on ways you can interact more effectively.

Volunteer for a new partnership opportunity—Consider getting involved with new groups both internally and externally. For example, look for a project or task force that means collaborating with another business unit or people from a different location, demographic, or functional area. Outside your organization, join a community task force or advocacy group to practice using partnership-building skills. Playing team games or sports is a great way to build partnerships. If possible, join a company or department team or league.

Work on fixing a broken partnership—Do you have a dysfunctional or unproductive partnership that has strong potential value? Try a fresh start. Let your partner know you value the partnership—and, of course, him or her as a partner. Candidly share your thoughts about what went wrong and invite the partner to give his or her perspective. Ask for another chance. If the partner agrees, seek ideas for improving (e.g., "What happened to make things fall apart?" and "If we start over, what could we do differently?"). Share your thoughts and feelings candidly. Also, be sure to maintain your partner's self-esteem—acknowledge past efforts as well as future contributions.

Get feedback on your partnership skills—Ask a trusted peer or leader to observe you as you work with a partner and provide specific feedback on the Key Actions for this competency. Ask your partners for feedback, too. Don't be satisfied with polite, evasive comments such as, "Everything's okay." If you sense that a partner is not fully satisfied, draw out specifics. For more formal partnerships, use a service partnership scorecard. Rate each other on a variety of agreed-upon standards. Typical scorecard items include:

- Technical expertise
- Communication
- Responsiveness
- Relationship Skills

4

Rating scales can be 1-5 or Does Not Meet/Meets/Exceeds Expectations. Exchange feedback, encourage open-ended comments, and set goals for improvement on both sides.

Help partners solve a problem—Sometimes partners simply cannot see eye to eye or make progress. If you work with a team that encompasses multiple partnerships, offer to assist if others can't reach agreement. Help them overcome an impasse by offering to facilitate or even mediate. Help partners share information in a balanced manner so the parties have adequate time for both "seek" and "tell." Establish what the partnership has to offer each party and remind them of the value often. Make sure meetings end with each party agreeing to clear next steps.

Support for developing Building Partnerships

Emotional Intelligence Essentials. Building partnerships is fundamentally an interpersonal endeavor, and productive partnerships are sustained through trust. Perhaps most important is involving your partners. Make sure to integrate the partners' perspectives, goals, and ideas into solutions. In problem solving and as you maintain the relationship over time, acknowledge your partners' contributions and accomplishments. Remind your partners that you value them.

Continuous Learning. Partnerships can be exciting, and they can teach you so much. They introduce you to new people, perspectives, and experiences. Show your investment in the relationship by learning more about your partners and their organization or area of expertise.

Driving for Results. Unlike social relationships, successful business partnerships are tied to business objectives and should produce measurable results. Your business partnerships should have clear expectations and plans to work toward mutually beneficial goals. Revitalize—or end—any stagnant or unproductive partnerships.

5 Business Acumen

Using economic, financial, market, and industry insights to contribute to effective business strategies and improve individual, team, and organizational results.

The Spirit of This Competency

Wouldn't we all like to be viewed as business experts? To have business acumen is to bring keen judgment to business-related decisions, but having that sort of expert ability is rarely innate. Rather, it's usually the result of combining experiential wisdom with sound business knowledge and a rational decision-making process. If you have business acumen, you can quickly and accurately size up opportunities or crises. You understand strategic direction, organizational functions, financial indicators, and current market conditions. You can cut through the "noise" of overwhelming—even conflicting—data to quickly decide what's viable.

Self-Insight Questions

How are you doing with Business Acumen right now? Ask yourself:

- How could I stay more up-to-date on current and future market trends and their impact on my business unit's strategy?

- How well do I leverage my business expertise to mitigate risks and improve results for my department or team?

- Am I using the right data sources to evaluate business opportunities and make better decisions?

- Do I understand how work gets done across the organization, not just in my functional area?

5

Key Actions: Building Blocks for Success

Key Actions are behaviors that work together to help you demonstrate this competency effectively.

Analyze—Use economic, financial, market, and industry information to identify trends and evaluate specific business opportunities.

Integrate—Compare economic, financial, market, and industry data from multiple sources to identify critical issues and determine how they might affect your team and the broader organization.

Understand business functions—Learn about the nature and interdependencies of your organization's functions (R&D, marketing, finance, operations, etc.) and processes.

Understand the industry—Learn more about the industry in which your organization operates (trends, customers, competition, market share, etc.).

Leverage your understanding—Use what you know about business functions, the industry, and your organization's performance to limit risk and maximize results for your department or team and the organization.

When you're demonstrating business acumen effectively, you'll notice:

People see you as a business expert.

- People ask you for advice. They see you as credible, and your unique experiences and insights can help them decide courses of action.
- People learn from your example and use your previous decisions and recommendations as a basis for their own decisions.
- Stakeholders across the organization trust that you understand and appreciate their varying agendas.
- You develop business plans collaboratively, so your plans meet your business partners' needs.

Your solutions address key business demands and opportunities.

- You can quickly assess the financial health of a business unit or organization by knowing a few key indicators.
- Your recommendations and decisions support your organization's business goals and strategic plans, save time or money, encourage creativity and innovation, and align with your systems, processes, and practices.
- You trust your instincts and perceptions and tap into your collective experiences to make recommendations quickly and confidently.
- You avoid making decisions based on hunches, intuition, or unsubstantiated data.
- You're in touch with what your customers want. You continuously scan the environment to hear their voices.

Your "risky" proposals pay off.

- Others might see your business recommendations as risky, but you know they are rooted in sound analysis.
- You're more willing than cautious colleagues to swiftly take advantage of key market opportunities.
- You determine risk based on diverse sectors and multiple perspectives rather than silos or single inputs (e.g., the economy, market share).

Critical Leadership Moments

As a leader, you face situations, or **Critical Leadership Moments,** that stretch your skills. Business Acumen can help you to:

Manage

▶ Manage the Risk Associated with Critical Business Decisions

▶ Identify New Business Directions

▶ Manage Information Overload

▶ Get Better Operational Results (quality, cost, efficiency)

Business Acumen is **essential** for success if you want to:

5

Manage the Risk Associated with Critical Business Decisions

To balance the risk and potential payoff when making crucial business decisions, focus on these **Key Actions:**

- **Understand business functions** across your organization to be aware of how decisions can affect stakeholders, processes, and operations.

- **Understand the industry** in which your organization operates to evaluate how proposed business decisions will differentiate you in the market and be received by your customers.

- **Leverage your understanding** of your business and industry to confidently make decisions that minimize risk and maximize results.

Also see the **Decision Making** competency to be even better prepared for this Critical Leadership Moment.

Identify New Business Directions

To use your understanding of what's happening in your business, industry, and market to propose strategic shifts, focus on these **Key Actions:**

- **Analyze** economic, financial, market, and industry information so you can spot trends and look for business opportunities.

- **Integrate** the information you gather to pinpoint the most critical issues and opportunities. What will they mean for your team and the broader organization?

- **Leverage your understanding** of the business landscape so you can see which opportunities might lead to the best results for your department, team, and organization.

Also see the **Driving Innovation** competency to be even better prepared for this Critical Leadership Moment.

Business Acumen will **boost** your success if you want to:

Manage Information Overload

While skills in **Decision Making** will help you to sort through and evaluate a vast amount of information, improving in Business Acumen can help you to detect trends that have the greatest bearing on your industry and organization.

Get Better Operational Results (quality, cost, efficiency)

While **Decision Making** is essential for creating processes and plans that will improve business outcomes, Business Acumen can help you balance operational demands with a broader, more strategic perspective. Your business acumen will also help you make better operational decisions as you track financial and productivity indicators and strive to improve them.

5

⚠ Common Mistakes

You can avoid common Business Acumen errors by paying attention to how people react to your efforts.

Under Actions

When you don't demonstrate the Key Actions for Business Acumen effectively, the results can be disappointing.

If you notice that:	You might be:	Try these quick remedies:
You miss business opportunities	**Refusing to take calculated risks**	• Increase your tolerance for experimentation and failure. Work with colleagues or mentors who challenge you to be bold. • Implement a plan in versions or stages if tackling a project or solution all at once feels overwhelming.
Your solutions don't have broad or lasting benefits	**Focusing too narrowly on your organization, industry, or location**	• Adopt a worldview and look at the bigger picture. Understanding how the global business and political landscape can support or undermine your business is essential to making effective business decisions. • Know the "upstream" and "downstream" effects of your decisions. Prepare others before you implement a decision and be aware of implications or consequences that might follow.
Your business case lacks robust data	**Missing opportunities to use technology-based analytical tools**	• Use software and big-data analysis tools to look for trends and spot opportunities you'd miss without sophisticated, unbiased data manipulation and visualization. • Read articles and research that provide current and predictive summaries of your industry, product, or service. • Avoid seeking only data that affirms your perceptions or intentions; look for contradictory data too.
Partners question or reject your recommendations	**Overlooking a variety of trusted perspectives**	• Part of having business savvy is knowing when to ask others for insights and when to reconsider things you overlooked or thought insignificant. Involving people from across the organization, including peers, direct reports, or your boss, can produce valuable, diverse perspectives.

5

Over Actions

When you demonstrate certain Business Acumen Key Actions at an extreme level, it can lead to poor results.

If you notice that:	You might be:	Try these quick remedies:
You make decisions too slowly or too late	Overanalyzing or gathering too much data	• Define the business problem you want to solve to determine what information is essential and what is interesting but irrelevant. • Realize that there is rarely a "perfect" solution for a complex business issue. Avoid continuing to seek data for an opportunity too urgent for lengthy comprehensive analysis.
Your plans work really well for some, but hardly at all for others	Too focused on one group's needs	• Take care not to overemphasize one organizational system, process, department, or function when the decision affects the whole organization. For example, focusing solely on the financial impact of a plan can disrupt operations, sales, or technology. • Make decisions with the organization's long-term strategy or goals in mind, as all functional areas and departments should be working toward those goals.
Others are questioning your judgment	Overly confident	• Solicit candid feedback about the impact of your decisions and use that feedback to improve. Otherwise, people will think you have little regard for the consequences of your decisions. • Create an advisory group of respected, experienced colleagues who can highlight areas of risk and threat (e.g., market readiness, resource preparedness, etc.) in your proposals. Assign a few the role of "devil's advocate."
Your solutions fail because of poor timing	Too eager to act	• Work with senior stakeholders to prioritize actions or solutions—and their timing—that will have the greatest impact on your business. What is the return on investment, how immediately is a solution needed, and what impact will it have on your business unit's strategy? What is the cost of acting sooner rather than later? When is the best time to get management support, secure resources, etc.?

Development Activities

Some of these activities will help you quickly address Critical Leadership Moments. Others require a greater investment of time and resources and can be part of your longer-term development plan. Choose the activities that work best for your goals.

▶▷▷ **Prepare for It...** Prepare for interactions in which your business acumen will be needed.

Understand how your business makes money—Review economic, financial, market, and industry data about your organization. You can read annual reports and go to shareholders' meetings. Compare your organization's performance to that of a benchmark organization or a competitor. Also, try web-based research tools to mine comparative data.

Learn more about the nature and interdependencies of business functions—How does business get done in your organization? Get familiar with supporting processes such as R&D, marketing, operations, engineering, etc. You could ask to join their team meetings and see their longer-term business plans.

Boost your industry knowledge and connections—What are your products? Who are your customers? Who's your competition? What are the latest advancements in your industry? To answer these questions cultivate a broad network of knowledgeable advisors and experts, in and outside your organization. For example:

- **Join** industry groups on social media.
- **Follow** expert bloggers.
- **Subscribe** to industry-related journals and newsletters.
- **Attend** networking events and educational/technical workshops.

Understand your organization's long- and short-term strategies—Building a network with senior leaders can help you learn more about the business planning process. Are you sure your team's activities and priorities align with the organization's direction?

Identify business growth opportunities and key market drivers—Which prospects have the greatest potential for your part of the organization? Partners in your organization who are closest to the customer, like Marketing and Sales, can help you decide as can customer feedback surveys and consumer focus group information. Reading customers' annual reports and industry-specific information can help you learn about their businesses.

Broaden your worldview—Learn how your organization fits into a broader economic and political landscape. For example, ask: What is happening in the world today? What does it mean for us and for other organizations? What has to happen first for us to achieve our desired results, and how can we set up the situation for success? Which factors can we control? What do we do next?

Take a finance or business course—Helpful classes will advance your knowledge and allow you to work on group projects or case studies.

▶▶▷ **Try It...** Practice using your business acumen skills.

Build a business plan—When creating a plan for a new venture, product, service, or approach to the business:

- **Collaborate** with someone who has built strong business plans in the past.
- **Conduct** a detailed analysis to determine your organization's competitive advantage (and where you can better differentiate in the market).
- **Conduct** an ROI analysis to see if the idea or proposal will be profitable.
- **Present** your analysis and plan to senior leaders and ask for feedback.

Read a competitor's annual report—Strategize how you would improve that organization's performance or construct a business plan that would beat your organization.

Recall situations in which you made decisions—Document your decision-making process. If you could make the decisions again, what would you do differently? What do you know now that you didn't know then? Where did you take or avoid risks? What lessons did you learn? Do you see any trends or tendencies? Consider keeping a journal of your insights, perceptions, and seminal experiences related to business decisions.

Test several approaches—How would you resolve a critical business issue aggressively versus conservatively? List the pros and cons of each approach.

Regularly review quantitative data—Create or locate reports, such as financials, balance sheets, budgets, and sales results, that give information on your areas of responsibility. An analytics software that displays data visually can help you to better interpret information, identify trends, and determine cause/effect relationships. Invite an objective colleague to review the results with you and ask for insights.

►►► Stretch It... Apply your business acumen skills in more challenging ways.

Volunteer for cross-functional opportunities or task forces—This is a good way to learn more about your organization and how the business makes money. Seek variety: Find an opportunity in which you're highly experienced and another where you have quite a bit to learn. Or try collaborating with an area, team, department, or organization that your group should be working with closely but is not. Start talking with key players from both sides and try to understand each other's key systems, processes, functions, and financials.

Take on a leadership role in an industry group or trade organization—If you aren't confident about tackling this assignment just yet, find a mentor or volunteer to co-chair an event or committee.

Join a community organization—You could volunteer for a community project that involves business activity, such as acquiring a building or negotiating a lease. Analyze the financial health of the organization and suggest ways to improve it. Offer to help plan and carry out a nonprofit's fund-raising efforts.

Get better at SWOT (strengths, weaknesses, opportunities, and threats) analysis—Use this detailed analysis to understand a business threat or opportunity and then to select the best strategy to address it.

Anticipate customer needs your organization doesn't fulfill—Do your customers—or potential customers—use products or services you don't provide? Brainstorm ways you could expand your offerings to meet more of your customers' needs.

Do a "postmortem" at the completion of a significant project or implementation—Ask peers and leaders for feedback on your analysis and decision-making skills.

Support for developing Business Acumen

Continuous Learning. Improving and maintaining your understanding of business requires that you keep learning and stay up-to-date in a rapidly changing business environment. Sometimes, this means exploring unfamiliar topics and situations.

Driving for Results. Making big shifts in business direction often entails risk; however, if you move too cautiously, you might miss opportunities. Be tenacious about improvement by challenging others to strive for more. Keep business initiatives moving by measuring progress and resetting priorities when necessary.

5

6 Coaching

Engaging an individual in developing and committing to an action plan that targets the specific behaviors, skills, or knowledge needed to ensure performance improvement or prepare for success in new responsibilities.

The Spirit of This Competency

This competency is about maximizing a person's performance by applying the right mix of interpersonal skills and leadership influence. In today's environment, you—as a coach—need to be proactive about driving optimal performance, not just with daily operations but with people too. As a coach, you inspire; you build people's skills, knowledge, confidence, and self-esteem. Whether helping someone overcome a performance challenge or preparing someone for a new, exciting opportunity, your coaching is key to building capability across the organization.

Self-Insight Questions

How are you doing at Coaching right now? Ask yourself:

- Do I use consistent, effective techniques to identify a person's gaps in knowledge, experience, and skills?

- How effectively do I provide feedback and guidance to help others excel in their current and future jobs? Do I balance seeking and telling?

- When coaching, do I communicate the need for behavior change in a compelling manner?

- What do I do to get people's commitment to performance plans and goals?

- Do I ensure that others feel valued and understood?

Key Actions: Building Blocks for Success

Key Actions are behaviors that work together to help you demonstrate this competency effectively.

Align expectations for the discussion—Describe the purpose and importance of the coaching session; check for understanding.

Define the performance challenge—Explain the need for improvement or preparation for a new opportunity; share specific examples.

Maintain motivation—Acknowledge the person's contributions and progress without minimizing challenges; empathize with concerns.

Engage and involve—Ask questions to further clarify the issues and their causes; collaboratively develop a plan by seeking and building upon the person's ideas.

Offer support—Provide assistance by sharing suggestions for improvement, development resources, positive models, or opportunities for experimentation; express confidence in the person.

Gain agreement—Emphasize the anticipated positive impact of planned actions; confirm the person's commitment.

Establish an action plan—Summarize the specific actions the person will take; assign clear accountability, timelines, and progress measures; monitor progress and results.

When you're coaching effectively, you'll notice:

Team members are performing at their highest levels.

- People proactively seek coaching and advice.
- You offer specific, immediate, and balanced feedback. You describe exactly what a person has done to be effective and seek or suggest what he or she could have done to be more effective.
- Team members are more self-aware, self-correcting, and independent. As a result, you can focus more time and energy on other responsibilities.
- Your staff are working to their full potential and not wasting time on unproductive or misdirected activities.

Coaching sessions are supportive and collaborative, not directive.

- You and your team don't dread coaching sessions. Instead, everyone looks forward to the opportunity to communicate candidly.
- People open up to you because you empathize with their positive and negative emotions.
- You listen and effectively balance seeking and telling.
- Your direct reports are invested in and committed to their development plans. They don't feel you've manipulated them into doing what you want.
- You offer your support at all times, not just when things are going well.
- You learn as much from others as they learn from you.

Coaching isn't reserved for performance problems.

- People aren't surprised by what you say about their performance and potential. You've made coaching routine, and you take advantage of every coachable moment.
- People feel prepared and motivated to take on new and challenging assignments because you've spent time coaching them for success.
- You recognize a job well done and celebrate others' accomplishments.

6

Critical Leadership Moments

As a leader, you face situations, or **Critical Leadership Moments,** that stretch your skills. Coaching can help you to:

Engage

▸ Coach a Person with a Performance Problem

▸ Prepare Someone for an Ambitious Assignment

▸ Empower Your Team

▸ Challenge Your Team to Stretch Their Performance

Coaching is **essential** for success if you want to:

Coach a Person with a Performance Problem

To help a person improve a challenging performance issue, focus on these **Key Actions:**

- **Define the performance challenge** and clearly explain the need for improvement. Be sure to share specific examples and explain the negative impact of the person's behavior.

- **Engage and involve** the person by asking questions to clarify the performance issues and their causes. Work together to develop an improvement plan. Seek and build on the other person's ideas.

- **Establish a plan** that summarizes the specific actions the individual will take to improve knowledge, skills, or behavior. Make sure accountability is clear. Agree on timelines and progress measures and set a follow-up date. Monitor the person's progress and results.

Also see the **Influencing** competency to be even better prepared for this Critical Leadership Moment.

Prepare Someone for an Ambitious Assignment

To help a team member or colleague succeed with a difficult task or challenging assignment, focus on these **Key Actions:**

- **Engage and involve** the person by asking questions. Identify any issues, concerns, or obstacles. Develop a plan by seeking and building upon the other person's ideas.

- **Offer support** so the person doesn't feel alone in tackling the challenge. Share suggestions for improvement, development resources, positive models, or opportunities for experimentation. Be sure to express confidence in the person.

- **Gain agreement** from the individual. Get their commitment by emphasizing how the plan you've developed together will have positive impact.

Also see **Delegation and Empowerment** competency to be even better prepared for this Critical Leadership Moment.

 Coaching will **boost** your success if you want to:

Empower Your Team

While **Delegation and Empowerment** is essential for building team commitment through meaningful work and motivational guidance, providing your team members with frequent feedback on their performance will help to continually build their skills and prepare them for challenging, new assignments.

Challenge Your Team to Stretch Their Performance

While **Guiding Team Success** is essential when creating a team environment that encourages team members to strive for excellence, it's also important that you provide one-on-one coaching. When you deliver clear feedback and direction, offer support, and boost your team members' confidence, you'll find that people are more likely to step out of their comfort zones and strive for ambitious performance goals.

6

⚠️ Common Mistakes

You can avoid common Coaching errors by paying attention to how people react to your efforts.

Under Actions

When you don't demonstrate the Key Actions for Coaching effectively, the results can be disappointing.

If you notice that:	You might be:	Try these quick remedies:
Your team isn't performing up to standard	**Missing coaching opportunities**	• Coach when you see the need. Don't wait to see if the person works things out alone. • Give positive feedback to encourage people to repeat behavior and to give them confidence as they tackle challenging assignments. • While quick instruction might solve an immediate problem, coaching helps to improve a person's longer-term capabilities.
Your coaching isn't effective with everyone	**Coaching the same way every time**	• Ask questions to clarify personal and practical needs, then tailor the action plan to the person's specific performance goals. • Base the amount of guidance you provide on the person's expertise, the difficulty of the task, and the consequences of failure.
Your coaching message isn't getting through	**Sugarcoating feedback**	• Sugarcoating feedback makes it meaningless. Give specific, behavioral feedback so the person understands why and how to improve. • Offer compelling rationale—including consequences and benefits—for change. Don't minimize the impact of the concern or inflate the person's potential.
You coach, but the team still struggles	**Assuming team members' understanding, commitment, and self-sufficiency**	• Be sure the person understands your recommendations, offers input to the action plan, and expresses buy-in. People are more likely to commit to a plan they helped to devise. • Check in regularly as the person works on improving. Anticipate obstacles and offer support as needed.

6

Over Actions

When you demonstrate certain Coaching Key Actions at an extreme level, it can lead to poor results.

If you notice that:	You might be:	Try these quick remedies:
People are upset after a coaching discussion	**Too critical**	• Be sensitive to others' feelings. Providing honest feedback is essential, but a large amount of corrective feedback can evoke hostility and inhibit productivity and creativity. • Provide accurate feedback; don't inflate consequences. Provide balanced feedback; praise and reinforce what others are doing right.
Your team feels disempowered	**Jumping in too soon or too much**	• Avoid dictating what the person should do. Encourage him or her to generate ways to improve, then build on those ideas and help shape them into an action plan. • Offer advice and support judiciously. Ask what the person needs; don't assume you know and then provide too much.
People aren't getting the expected results	**Creating weak performance-improvement plans**	• Plans for enhanced performance should include goals that are SMART: specific, measurable, accountable, relevant, and time bound. • After planning, don't check in too frequently; you'll risk undermining trust. Give the person adequate time to make progress.
People are confused about expectations	**Inadvertently increasing performance standards**	• Be sure expectations are clear, consistent, and realistic. Update formal job descriptions and performance expectations as roles evolve.

6

Development Activities

Some of these activities will help you quickly address Critical Leadership Moments. Others require a greater investment of time and resources and can be part of your longer-term development plan. Choose the activities that work best for your goals.

▶▷▷ Prepare for It... Prepare for coaching opportunities.

Analyze who, when, and why you coach—How you can be more effective? Ask yourself:

- Am I coaching only low-performing team members? Top performers need coaching too and can often do much more if given the right guidance and support.

- Do I allow certain situations to persist? If so, you'll face more difficult conversations later. Coach early and temper your message based on the urgency of the situation and the potential consequences.

- Am I abdicating coaching? If you rely on top performers to coach others through peer feedback, tension can result. Leverage top performers as mentors, but don't hold them accountable for their teammates' performance.

- Am I nitpicking some people's performance? Coach fairly and apply expectations consistently; otherwise, you can erode team morale. Set routine coaching conversations with everyone—same time and frequency.

Get to know your team—Your coaching message won't get through if it feels "canned" or generic. You want to coach the whole team, but some people will be more ready than others. Size up your team; look for group trends but also individual preferences. Are your direct reports:

- Aware of their strengths and development needs?
- Involved in development planning?
- Motivated to improve their performance?
- Aware of their contributions to the group's success?
- Confident that you'll support them when they face performance challenges?
- Recognized for performance improvement and success?

If you aren't sure, ask, using these questions to personalize your coaching. Make sure people know that you're working to understand and meet their unique personal and practical needs.

Remove common performance roadblocks—Where does your team tend to struggle, miss deadlines, get frustrated, or run into conflict? Are any policies or procedures getting in the way? What can you do to remove the roadblocks before they affect performance? Do you need resources or funding? Do organizational or team priorities shift too often? Discuss recurring obstacles with your manager. Together, think about what you can change to empower your team to make decisions or access the resources they need to do their jobs effectively.

Build a library of skill-building resources—Most coaching conversations result in an action plan or goal, and to reach those goals people need support. That support—especially if it's geared toward increasing knowledge or technical expertise—might come in the form of books, articles, and websites. As you come across development resources, organize them by topic in an electronic folder. Review the sources occasionally to make sure they're still current and relevant.

▶▶▷ Try It... Practice coaching.

Create a culture of development—What can you do to create a safe environment for continually building skills and taking risks in learning?

- Prioritize development. That might mean allowing people with demanding workloads to also take on skill-enhancing assignments. Make learning and development a team and individual goal.

- Be a proactive coach. Look for ways people can stretch their skills and try new things. Know your team members' goals and aspirations and ask them, "What would you like to work on/learn next?" Don't let development become a hassle for the team—secure resources and support and don't "dump and run" when giving assignments.

- Help the team expect and accept feedback. Take advantage of every coachable moment—you don't have to wait for a formal coaching session.

- Express confidence in team members' abilities. Sometimes all people need to hear is "I know you can do it."

Give specific, balanced feedback—When giving feedback:

- Time it right. Is the person in a receptive mind-set? Are you in an open mind-set to give feedback? Do you have enough time to provide details and examples? If not, find a better time but give feedback as close to the performance as possible.

- Be clear. Compliments won't help the person know what to keep doing, and gentle hints won't send the message about what needs to change. Instead, describe exactly what the person has done to be effective or exactly what he or she could have done better, using behavioral examples or quantitative evidence. Be candid about implications and consequences for the person, team, or organization.

- Balance your message. If you're sharing mostly feedback for improvement, be sure also to recognize things the person has done well to improve the person's motivation and confidence.

Practice equal-opportunity coaching—Schedule regular updates with each team member and offer coaching every time. Offer your best people the same time and attention as those who might be struggling. These routine one-on-ones will help you avoid the "You have a minute?" quick chats that rarely encompass all the Coaching Key Actions.

Watch for assumptions and biases—Base your feedback on behavioral observations and objective data. Use job descriptions to define performance expectations rather than your personal preferences. During your coaching conversations, find out more about the person's motives, attitudes, or thoughts. Otherwise, you won't have a clear picture of what someone has done or has the potential to do.

Formalize performance goals and plans—Work with the person to establish a clear plan for getting where he or she wants (or needs) to be. Use the SMART framework to set goals that are specific, measurable, accountable, relevant, and time bound. Don't be afraid to set stretch goals, but be realistic. Goals that are too ambitious can erode motivation and self-confidence. Agree on when you'll follow up and on how much progress is expected by then.

Coach from good to great—Is it possible that some of your best performers don't feel challenged in their everyday work? If you coach your team to build their depth and breadth of knowledge, you'll help them be stronger all-around performers, increasing their value to the team and the organization. Look for stretch assignments (project teams, task forces, committees) and try assigning a task to someone who will learn from it rather than to an expert.

Continually build trust—Your coaching will be most effective when you and the person you're coaching trust each other. Build trust by involving people, sharing information, empathizing with their concerns, asking questions to gain understanding, and maintaining their esteem. Be forthcoming with information and share your thoughts and experiences—even your development objectives. If you point out a mistake, maintain esteem by acknowledging the difficulty of the task and recognizing what the person is doing well. Do the nonverbals say the person is uncomfortable or nervous? Use trust-building behaviors to build rapport and ease any tension.

Celebrate success—Acknowledge wins along the way—no need to wait until someone has met every objective. Be specific about what the person has done well. How can you publicize—but not exaggerate—success? Consider making recognition a standing agenda item at team meetings or use organizationwide communication tools to celebrate significant team achievements.

▶▶▶ **Stretch It...** Apply coaching in more challenging ways.

Create "superteams"—Engage high performers in exciting assignments that stretch their skills. Gather a few high performers into a superteam and encourage them to experiment and break boundaries as they solve a challenging problem. Provide time, funding, and—most important—your guidance. Advocate for their efforts within the organization and celebrate their success.

Coach beyond your team—Coach a peer or a project team working on something outside your area but where you can offer guidance. Coach or mentor outside work too, for a community group or sports team. Look for parallels between the community situation and your work. If you run into difficulties with new people, cultures, or policies, identify which skills you can improve and incorporate them into your personal development plan.

Ask provocative questions—Clarifying information is key to coaching, but if your questioning sometimes feels like an interrogation, try asking more thought-provoking questions ("Imagine if _____. What would happen?" or "What is the best/worst possible outcome and why?"). These questions can:

- Help you gain a more complete view of a problem or opportunity and thus a more effective solution.
- Discover any assumptions getting in the way of optimal performance.
- Envision the ideal future state. From there, you can work backward to define the performance improvements and goals needed to get there.

Evaluate your coaching style—Try these approaches:

- Ask an expert to observe you coaching someone and then give you specific feedback, including suggestions for improvement.
- Administer a multirater survey focused on coaching to direct reports, colleagues, and your manager.
- With permission, make a video as you coach a direct report. Watch the video and evaluate your performance. Commit to doing two or three things differently in the next coaching discussion.
- Think back to the best coaches you've known. Write down what they did to be so influential, then reflect on what you can do be more like them.

Rally your own team of mentors—Find people in your organization or industry who are known for excellent coaching skills. What can you learn from them? When you network with colleagues, discuss their coaching style. What challenges do they face, and how do they overcome them? What approaches do they think are most effective?

Be a role model—Coaches need coaching too, so be a model for continuous performance improvement and career growth. Have a development plan and communicate often with your coach or manager. Share your plan with your team and build trust by sharing the challenges you have encountered.

Support for developing Coaching

Emotional Intelligence Essentials. Coaching conversations can be uncomfortable. The person you're coaching might feel vulnerable or defensive. While your style might be to get straight to the point, the person will be more open to your coaching and more likely to improve if you share your message in a safe, collaborative, and supportive environment.

Continuous Learning. Be a model for ongoing skill development. Let your team see you learn something new and apply those skills to a challenging assignment. Be as accountable for development as anyone on the team. Staying current on industry and technical knowledge can also help as you provide guidance and direction, sharing what you've learned to build the team's capabilities.

Driving for Results. Everyday demands can get in the way of focused development. Stretch goals and development plans can be ignored or deprioritized when time and resources are limited. When you coach, hold people accountable for their action plans and work to eliminate obstacles and distractions.

7 Creating an Inclusive Environment

Making decisions and initiating action to leverage the capabilities and insights of people with diverse backgrounds, cultures, styles, abilities, and motivation.

The Spirit of This Competency

Due to shifting workplace demographics and an interdependent global economy, you'll most likely lead and collaborate with people from diverse cultures, styles, and backgrounds. How can you leverage those differences to engage all team members and achieve top results? Create an environment in which you and your team seek and value a wide range of talents, experiences, and perspectives. Advocating for diversity goes beyond being more inclusive; it means trying to understand the world from all possible angles so you can be informed and innovative. Nurturing diversity makes the best use of people's talents, leading to superior ideas, decisions, and productivity.

Self-Insight Questions

How are you doing at Creating an Inclusive Environment right now? Ask yourself:

- Do others see me as an advocate for diversity? Why or why not?

- What have I done to learn more about people from different cultures and backgrounds?

- What actions have I taken to ensure that policies and practices leverage the capabilities of individuals with diverse cultures, styles, abilities, and backgrounds?

- When others demonstrate racist, sexist, or inappropriate behavior related to another person's differences, how do I respond?

Key Actions: Building Blocks for Success

Key Actions are behaviors that work together to help you demonstrate this competency effectively.

Seek understanding—Gather information to learn about people from other cultures and backgrounds.

Use diversity as an advantage—Seek and use ideas and insights from diverse sources and individuals; align team members' unique talents with the most relevant responsibilities.

Convey respect—Use language and behavior that enhance the dignity of people from diverse backgrounds; examine your biases to avoid stereotypical responses.

Champion diversity—Take action to increase diversity (e.g., by recruiting and developing people with varied backgrounds); confront racist, sexist, or inappropriate behavior; challenge exclusionary practices.

When you're creating an inclusive environment effectively, you'll notice:

Team members respect others' differences.

- People view differences as assets and are comfortable partnering across different functions, cultures, and teams.

- Team members have a strong sense of belonging, and new people easily assimilate into the team's culture. Despite their differences, everyone feels part of a group with a shared purpose.

- A climate of open communication and trust exists. People feel free to express their differences and enjoy discussing them.

Championing diversity is improving your effectiveness as a leader.

- You don't need to plan diversity or affirmative action initiatives because your everyday leadership decisions and actions promote inclusion.

- You leverage the unique talents of your team members.

- You recruit and develop people with diverse backgrounds and offer opportunities based on objective data, not subjective opinions.

Optimizing diversity is an integral part of your team's way of working.

- Team members evaluate information with an open mind rather than defaulting to assumptions and stereotypes.

- Your team considers how decisions will affect all parties and includes representatives of diverse groups in the decision-making process. As a result, team members gain fresh perspectives, uncover new information, and make more accurate decisions.

- The team proposes many unexpected yet sound ideas thinking "outside the box."

- You facilitate respectful, constructive disagreements and engage differing perspectives as your team makes decisions.

7

Critical Leadership Moments

As a leader, you face situations, or **Critical Leadership Moments,** that stretch your skills. Creating an Inclusive Environment can help you to:

Partner
▶ Strengthen Relationships with Your Peers
▶ Expand Your Business Network

Engage
▶ Be a Diversity Advocate

Manage
▶ Consider People's Differences as an Advantage

Creating an Inclusive Environment is **essential** for success if you want to:

Be a Diversity Advocate

To build a team culture that respects and celebrates people's differences, focus on these **Key Actions:**

- **Use diversity** as an advantage by building diverse teams that match peoples' unique talents and motivations with relevant responsibilities. Offer development and stretch opportunities to people from a variety of backgrounds.

- **Convey respect** to create an environment that enhances the dignity of people from all backgrounds. Model the behaviors you want others to demonstrate, avoiding your own biases.

- **Champion diversity** by promoting the benefits of considering different points of view and by challenging practices that exclude others. Watch for and confront racist, sexist, or inappropriate behavior.

Also see the **Guiding Team Success** competency to be even better prepared for this Critical Leadership Moment.

Consider People's Differences as an Advantage

To make better decisions by including others' diverse perspectives and experiences, focus on these **Key Actions:**

- **Seek understanding** by learning more about people from other cultures and backgrounds. This will help you consider other perspectives as you address problems and opportunities.

- **Use diversity as an advantage** by seeking insights from people with varied experiences as you make decisions and promote innovation.
- **Champion diversity** on your team by recruiting people with varied backgrounds. Look for opportunities to advocate for diverse viewpoints and more inclusive practices.

Also see the **Decision Making** competency to be even better prepared for this Critical Leadership Moment.

 Creating an Inclusive Environment will **boost** your success if you want to:

Strengthen Relationships with Your Peers

While **Building Partnerships** is essential for forming collaborative internal relationships, if you encourage inclusion people from all backgrounds will feel safe disclosing their unique ideas and talents. They'll know their perspectives and contributions are valued.

Expand Your Business Network

While **Building Partnerships** is essential for initiating new business contacts, if you reach out with an inclusive approach, your new contacts will be more likely to share unique experiences and talents that can broaden your perspective and boost your capability.

7

⚠️ Common Mistakes

You can avoid common Creating an Inclusive Environment errors by paying attention to how people react to your efforts.

Under Actions

When you don't demonstrate the Key Actions for Creating an Inclusive Environment effectively, the results can be disappointing.

If you notice that:	You might be:	Try these quick remedies:
Other teams are more innovative and effective	**Disregarding individual differences**	• Realize that differences among people are critical for your team's success. Model valuing diversity by discussing individual differences as opposed to denying or ignoring them. Use everyone's unique abilities to their best advantage. • Learn about or immerse yourself in new cultures. Work at being self-aware, so you don't unintentionally alienate people from other backgrounds.
Your team lacks people from varied backgrounds	**Discouraging diversity**	• When building project teams, involve people from diverse backgrounds. Look for biases in your evaluation criteria and decisions—it's common to favor those who are similar to you. • Uncover hidden potential by creating opportunities for people from groups underrepresented in important roles. Consider groups, functional areas, and locations not typically viewed as rich sources of talent.
People are overly cautious when interacting with you	**Disrespecting others**	• Examine your biases to avoid stereotypical or derogatory responses that can destroy trust. Show regard for other cultures with your words and actions. • Show you value others' concerns by getting their buy-in for plans and ideas. Encourage input with your body language by smiling, leaning forward, and maintaining eye contact.
Team tensions are building	**Avoiding confronting others' biases**	• When biases surface, take the opportunity to challenge assumptions and advocate for the benefits of diversity. • Confront stereotypes and prejudice directly. Ignoring or tolerating racist, sexist, or other exclusionary behavior enables similar behavior in others.

7

Over Actions

When you demonstrate certain Creating an Inclusive Environment Key Actions at an extreme level, it can lead to poor results.

If you notice that:	You might be:	Try these quick remedies:
People from different backgrounds aren't engaged	**Overemphasizing differences**	• Acknowledge similarities as well as differences when discussing other cultures and backgrounds. Exaggerating differences can make people feel like outcasts. Build trust by disclosing appropriate information about yourself. • Use discretion when asking questions about other people's backgrounds to avoid making the other person feel defensive. Look for nonverbal cues to gauge the person's reaction.
Stakeholders don't support your team's ideas	**Championing only the most diverse ideas**	• Realize that "different" might not be better in some situations. Sure, it's important to consider many perspectives and keep an open mind, but advance the most suitable ideas, diverse or not.
Team members don't trust you	**Overcompensating for bias**	• Make effective use of diverse capabilities and insights by giving honest feedback. Balance positive feedback with feedback for improvement. • Be aware of your biases but don't compensate by being overly lenient with people from diverse backgrounds. Others might distrust or resent you for it.
Certain groups resent your diversity efforts	**Singling out specific minority groups**	• Promote broader cultural diversity. Seek perspectives from representatives of various minority groups. • Expand your definition of diversity beyond gender, age, religion, ethnicity, or sexual orientation. Recognize and leverage the differences that come from people's personalities and educational, professional, or functional backgrounds.

7

Development Activities

Some of these activities will help you quickly address Critical Leadership Moments. Others require a greater investment of time and resources and can be part of your longer-term development plan. Choose the activities that work best for your goals.

▶▷▷ Prepare for It... Prepare for opportunities to create an inclusive environment.

Broaden your exposure—Increased exposure to more diverse experiences will make it easier for you and your team to understand and value individual differences. Browse international business and industry websites, blogs, and publications. Explore industries, business cultures, regions, and fields outside your areas of expertise. Exchange ideas and explore ways your team can apply their observations. Ask: What new relationships could we initiate within and outside our organization to expand our team's perspective?

Research unfamiliar cultures—Before meeting with people from another country, research its business culture. You'll need to be particularly aware of your biases so you don't judge other cultures and unintentionally alienate people. Discussions between people from different backgrounds or perspectives can often include gaps in communication. Always check your understanding of the other person's responses to prevent misunderstandings.

Increase your self-awareness—Increasing your diversity awareness can be challenging because often people won't point out your missteps, and you might not realize the negative effects of your words or actions. These are your blind spots. Watch for subtle clues, such as facial expressions or body language, that indicate you have transgressed cultural norms or offended someone. If you see negative reactions, ask yourself what you might be saying or doing to cause them.

Identify your biases or stereotypes—Everyone has biases, and many of them are unconscious—they're the shortcuts our brains take when processing information. These shortcuts are useful for increasing efficiency, but they can lead us to reach quick judgments and inaccurate conclusions. Work at recognizing when your judgments are based on someone's appearance or background rather than the merits of his or her ideas or results. Ask a trusted friend or colleague to share observations about your approach. Don't get defensive; instead, listen carefully and, together, identify ways to manage your biases.

Try It... Practice creating an inclusive environment.

Build more inclusive teams—Recruit employees with unique skill sets and perspectives that supplement your team's current capabilities. To decrease bias in hiring and promotion decisions, define success objectively—based on required knowledge, skills, and abilities—and compare each candidate's qualifications to those standards. Involve several evaluators in personnel decisions to view each candidate from multiple perspectives and to decrease the impact of individual biases.

Show that you value diversity—Model a positive attitude toward differing perspectives. React objectively to others' ideas—even those you don't agree with—and explore suggestions fully. If people with different viewpoints are quiet, ask for their opinions, show you value their insights, and build on their ideas. On the flip side, examine whether you're inadvertently discouraging people from sharing divergent perspectives (perhaps by not listening or by criticizing). Work to eliminate these behaviors.

Seek alternative perspectives—When solving problems or making decisions, seek input from a variety of colleagues. Consider why you tend to rely on certain internal experts, and then ask opinions of others who don't fit this mold. Invite the opinions of people from multiple levels, functions, and regions, including people who aren't familiar with the situation and might have a unique perspective. A good way to increase communication across diverse groups is by using social media channels and team collaboration tools that allow people to build on one another's ideas.

Treat diversity as a business imperative—Adopt inclusion as a critical business strategy and develop tangible tactics for championing individual differences. Communicate to your team and other leaders the ways a more diverse workforce could help your organization be a more competitive and desirable place to work. Understand the difference between an inclusive environment and affirmative action. Affirmative action programs are only the first step. You should support diversity initiatives not only to comply with legal requirements, but also because they'll make your organization more effective.

Recognize and reward diversity efforts—Set up formal and informal ways to reward people for contributions to diversity goals. Reward ideas that challenge the majority's view, publicly champion divergent perspectives, and advocate for people whose potential is being overlooked. If your organization has diversity initiatives, take accountability for advancing them through goals in team performance plans. Track progress and link results to performance evaluations and reward systems

>>> **Stretch It...** Create an inclusive environment in more challenging ways.

Expand your understanding of diversity in the workplace—Research websites, books, and articles to find out how other organizations have developed a diverse workforce and how their initiatives affected business outcomes. What aspects could you apply to your team?

Take responsibility for promoting diversity—Set up or participate in employee focus groups, diversity councils, networking groups, or corporate or business unit advisory committees. Initiate dialogs with minority groups to learn about their experiences. Identify problem areas and list tactics for increasing diversity and share them with appropriate leaders. Survey your work group to assess opinions about diversity. Ask: "How do you feel about diversity in our work group?" "Is it all that it should be?" Then advocate for diversity initiatives to address any perceived weaknesses the survey reveals.

Involve yourself and others in diversity training—These classes build awareness and promote open communication about issues related to individual differences. Participating can help you see your biases and blind spots in how you treat others. You might realize that actions you think are benign have adverse effects.

Explore opportunities to join a diverse team—Look for project teams that include people from different functions, regions, or levels to expose you and your team to other perspectives and ideas. For example, involve your team in plans to introduce a new process or procedure across the organization. Take on a role that's outside your expertise or that applies your knowledge within a group of people with backgrounds unfamiliar to you. Learn about people's backgrounds before engaging with them.

Participate in a community organization that champions the cause of a minority group—Select a group that will expose you to individuals who are very different from you (e.g., child mentoring programs, a women's shelter, immigrant support services, or a senior living facility).

Support for developing Creating an Inclusive Environment

Emotional Intelligence Essentials. Creating an inclusive team environment requires self-awareness as well as interpersonal sensitivity. Examine your biases and assumptions about people with backgrounds different from yours. Be sensitive in your discussions by asking thoughtful questions, listening carefully, and empathizing as others share their concerns and issues. Maintain and enhance people's self-esteem by showing that you value their involvement and unique perspectives, even when you don't see eye-to-eye.

Adaptability. Having a flexible mind-set will ease your work with people who are very different from you. Adjust your work style so you can collaborate when differences create barriers. Show others that you're ready to include new people, consider different perspectives, and try fresh solutions.

Continuous Learning. Find ways to learn about people, cultures, and knowledge areas outside your expertise. Step beyond your comfort zone. You'll learn to think about problems and opportunities from new perspectives that can lead to unique and more effective solutions.

7

8 Decision Making

Identifying and understanding problems and opportunities by gathering, analyzing, and interpreting information; generating alternatives, then choosing and implementing the best course of action.

The Spirit of This Competency

It's been said that every person makes 35,000 decisions each day, and many of them happen at work. The decisions you make as a leader reach beyond you; they also affect your team and your organization. Making decisions can mean walking a fine line: Sometimes you have too much information, sometimes not enough. You should seek input and consider all viable options, but is there something you're missing? What if you take action, and what if you don't? Every decision has consequences, and some decisions involve quite a bit of risk. Leaders need to strike a balance between cautiously conducting a thorough analysis and courageously taking effective, decisive, and timely action.

Self-Insight Questions

How are you doing at Decision Making right now? Ask yourself:

- Am I collecting the right information to help me make the most effective decisions?

- What methods do I use to organize data so I can interpret it accurately?

- Do I involve the appropriate people at each step in the decision-making process?

- Do I list alternatives and evaluate the implications of each before choosing the best one?

Key Actions: Building Blocks for Success

Key Actions are behaviors that work together to help you demonstrate this competency effectively.

Identify problems and opportunities—Recognize problems and opportunities and determine whether action is needed.

Gather information—Recognize the need for and collect information to better understand problems and opportunities.

Interpret information—Integrate information from a variety of sources to detect trends, associations, and cause-effect relationships.

Generate alternatives—Develop relevant options for addressing problems and opportunities.

Evaluate alternatives and risks—Assess options against clear decision criteria while considering implications and consequences.

Choose an effective option—Select the most viable option from a set of alternatives.

Commit to action—Implement decisions or initiate action with appropriate urgency.

Consider others' perspectives—Involve others throughout the decision-making process to obtain better information, generate alternatives, and ensure buy-in to the resulting decisions.

When you're making decisions effectively, you'll notice:

Very little, if any, controversy surrounds the quality of your decisions.

- You make decisions that consider both the organization's and your team's needs. As a result, your team respects organizational values and works to accomplish strategic goals.
- You don't make ineffective decisions. Others might prefer a different solution or view the problem differently, but no one can dispute your judgment.
- You model effective decision making and notice your team's decision-making skills improving, perhaps leading you to delegate more decision-making authority.
- You calculate the risks involved in your decision and seek others' feedback on the solution. You then revise your decision accordingly.

Others show faith in your decision-making ability.

- People often ask for your opinion when they're making decisions because they value your analytical skills and sound judgment.
- Your history of making sound business decisions leads your superiors to trust your decision-making abilities and feel less need to be involved in the process.
- You communicate your decisions to stakeholders before implementing them. This allows you and others to evaluate the impact on other parts of the business and to make contingency plans.

You boost team efficiency and morale by making sound, timely decisions.

- You are patient enough to listen to and gather data from others, but decisive enough to act. You don't drag out the process.
- You quickly grasp the root of the problem and stay focused on those core issues. You simplify the process by identifying the most important decision criteria.
- You consider and weigh the risks before investing time in your analysis.
- You quickly create and evaluate a range of alternatives and their potential consequences before making your decision.
- You involve others, as appropriate, in the decision-making process to optimize operational impact, morale, and the team's commitment to implementing the decision.

8

Critical Leadership Moments

As a leader, you face situations, or **Critical Leadership Moments,** that stretch your skills. Decision Making can help you to:

Manage

▶ Find the Best Solution Despite Limited Information

▶ Manage information Overload

▶ Consider People's Differences as an Advantage

▶ Get Better Operational Results (quality, cost, efficiency)

▶ Manage the Risk Associated with Critical Business Decisions

Decision Making is **essential** for success if you want to:

Find the Best Solution Despite Limited Information

To arrive at solid solutions to problems, even when information is incomplete, focus on these **Key Actions:**

- **Gather information** strategically and purposefully. If time or resources are limited, look for the most credible, comprehensive, and recent sources. Carefully weigh subjective opinions against objective facts.

- **Interpret information** across various sources to detect trends, associations, and cause-effect relationships. Recurring themes can help you identify and act on the root cause of a problem or find the biggest potential payoff to an opportunity.

- **Generate alternatives** and brainstorm several options. Even with limited information, you can increase your odds of making a good decision by devising and vetting several possible solutions.

Also see the **Driving Innovation** competency to be even better prepared for this Critical Leadership Moment.

Manage Information Overload

To sort through and evaluate a vast amount of information to enable quick decision making, focus on these **Key Actions:**

- **Gather information** in a focused way. Identify in advance what information you'll need and avoid allowing "interesting, but not relevant" information to distract you.

- **Interpret information** to distill abundant or overwhelming data into simple categories. Avoid analysis paralysis by organizing the information (i.e., look for trends, associations, and cause-effect relationships). Decide what information and conclusions are most reliable, then prioritize the most useful.

8

- **Commit to action** so you and your team can quickly implement decisions or initiate action. There will always be more information available; get comfortable making a judgment call, sometimes sooner than you might prefer.

Also see the **Business Acumen** competency to be even better prepared for this Critical Leadership Moment.

Get Better Operational Results (quality, cost, efficiency)

To create processes and plans and make decisions to improve business outcomes, focus on these **Key Actions:**

- **Consider others' perspectives** because sometimes those closest to the problem understand it best and might propose creative solutions. Involving others throughout the decision-making process (rather than informing them after you make the decision) helps you gather better information, generate more viable alternatives, and ensure buy-in to the resulting decisions.

- **Evaluate alternatives and risks** because most proposed solutions will come with implications and consequences. Use consistent and clear decision criteria so you consider alternatives objectively against the expected outcomes.

- **Commit to action** because the longer you deliberate, the worse the situation can get. Establish metrics to quickly tell if your decision is making a difference. Better to decide, measure, and adjust than delay taking action.

Also see the **Business Acumen** competency to be even better prepared for this Critical Leadership Moment.

8

 Decision Making will **boost** your success if you want to:

Consider People's Differences as an Advantage

While **Creating an Inclusive Environment** helps you to create a team culture that celebrates diversity, it also can enhance your decision making. Chances are, you have a subjective perspective on the problems and opportunities facing your team. Seek a variety of viewpoints and invite a diverse group to participate in problem solving. With broader input, you're more likely to find the best solution.

Manage the Risk Associated with Critical Business Decisions

While **Business Acumen** is essential for understanding your industry and market, tactical decision making also helps to manage business risk. Your decisions affect your team's processes and operations; however, they also can have implications for the organization's longer-term viability, profitability, or market position. Look beyond the short-term payoff or actions that will get immediate (but perhaps not sustainable) results. Consider the organization's—not just your team's—goals as key criteria for your decisions.

⚠ Common Mistakes

You can avoid common Decision Making errors by paying attention to how people react to your efforts.

Under Actions

When you don't demonstrate the Key Actions for Decision Making effectively, the results can be disappointing.

If you notice that:	You might be:	Try these quick remedies:
Problems linger, despite efforts to fix them	**Addressing symptoms, not the root cause**	• Step back and view the problem objectively. Gather and integrate information and keep asking "why" until you get to the root cause of the problem.
Problems are addressed quickly but not necessarily effectively	**Too eager to accept the first idea**	• Consider the implications of each alternative, especially the first one that comes to mind or the obvious one. • Avoid a problem-solving process that defaults to tradition or status quo. More analysis and fresh perspectives might uncover an opportunity for aggressive change or bold solutions.
People aren't supporting your solutions	**Making decisions in isolation**	• Seek others' insights. Check your facts and review the situation with at least one other person who has a different perspective. • Realize that you don't have to (and shouldn't!) make every decision yourself. Delegate decisions and involve direct reports in gathering information or generating alternatives. • Communicate the rationale for your decision, especially to those affected by it and in politically sensitive or emotionally charged situations. • Avoid actions that seem rebellious or self-serving. Align decisions with the organization's strategy and values.
You hesitate to commit	**Failing to take firm, timely action**	• Don't wait for someone else to take the lead in resolving problems. • Have the confidence to choose and advocate for the solution. It's your job to make the call, not to placate people, avoid controversy, or be liked. • Move quickly—and courageously—on communicating to the team and securing resources before rumors start.

8

Over Actions

When you demonstrate certain Decision Making Key Actions at an extreme level, it can lead to poor results.

If you notice that:	You might be:	Try these quick remedies:
You miss your window of opportunity	**Taking too long to assess the situation**	• Match the volume of analysis to the complexity and impact of the decision. If you analyze for too long, your information might be obsolete by the time you make a decision. • Realize that perfect decisions are rare, and continued data gathering and analysis aren't likely to yield perfection.
Solutions are conservative and lack creativity	**Overly risk averse**	• Be open to risk. Making "safe" decisions over and over means your team will take few bold or creative actions, thereby stifling innovation. • Evaluate risks based on facts, constraints, and probable consequences. Your decision criteria can change for each decision. Don't be distracted by past failures. Big risks sometimes lead to big rewards.
You delay decisions or miss deadlines	**Seeking too much input**	• Carefully consider who should be involved in the decision-making process and how much involvement each should have. Over-involving others can cause delays and missed deadlines. • Ask yourself why so many resources are involved. Are you trying to please everyone or involve people who see things your way? Set a specific amount of time for gathering input, then a non-negotiable deadline for choosing and implementing a course of action.
Your decisions are quick but not thorough	**Operating with an unfounded sense of urgency**	• Identify what needs to be decided right away and what can wait. Not everything is critical. Some problems take longer to define and investigate. • Follow a deliberate and comprehensive decision-making process rather than jumping to conclusions or accepting the first idea as the best. Instead, gather and integrate information, formulate clear decision criteria, generate alternatives, and then carefully consider the implications of each option before taking action.

8

Development Activities

Some of these activities will help you quickly address Critical Leadership Moments. Others require a greater investment of time and resources and can be part of your longer-term development plan. Choose the activities that work best for your goals.

▶▷▷ Prepare for It... Prepare for decision-making opportunities.

Plan to involve others in the decision-making process—Take an inventory of your circle. Keep a list of people affected by your decisions. Who's upstream, and who's downstream? Reference and prioritize that list when you make a decision. Review the list periodically (resources shift often) and keep those people and/or departments involved and informed. Also, while it's good to involve people close to the problem, build a network of objective resources who are likely to see a problem through a different lens.

Determine decision criteria—Even if you don't face an immediate decision, identify a set of decision criteria. For example, what are you or your team accountable for? Are there employee, team, or group metrics? What performance goals and objectives do you have as a leader? Perhaps you need to keep team morale, efficiency, or profitability at a certain level. Establish and stick to decision criteria that will help you meet or exceed those goals. Check all alternatives against those criteria.

Find out early what might get in your way—Identify potential roadblocks. First, gauge your team's receptivity to a proposed idea and find out how prepared they are for the ensuing actions or tasks. Ask your team to share—perhaps through a survey or candid conversation—their common pain points (such as what's dragging down morale, which processes aren't efficient, or what makes their work challenging). Identify potential barriers or incorrect assumptions before you propose an idea, or better yet, before you begin generating alternatives. Do the same with other stakeholders, such as peers and other departments.

Identify reliable and current sources of information—Create a personal "wiki" of sources, sites, people, studies, research, professional journals, news magazines, blogs, social media, and business newspapers. Follow industry thought leaders on social media and set reminders to view the latest posts and research, even if you don't face an impending decision. While external sources can provide excellent objective insights, how can you communicate frequently with internal stakeholders? For example, find out what reports, surveys, or studies Human Resources or Finance might provide.

▶▶▷ **Try It...** Practice your decision-making skills.

Do something now—Don't wait until you have to fix a problem; take action as soon as you see signs of trouble. While it might be tempting to wait to see if a situation improves without your intervention, taking even small steps early can make a difference.

Take a new and different look at data—Experiment with software and databases that specialize in data collection, management, and analysis. These tools can make complex data more understandable and help you to compare and contrast information. Look for options that offer data visualization or graphical displays (tables, charts, diagrams) to simplify information, find trends, and reach conclusions.

Keep asking "why?"—When analyzing a problem, determine the root cause. Keep asking why, perhaps using the interrogative technique of the "five why's." Use the information from one answer as the basis for the next question and do this until you've asked "why?" five times. You'll uncover related information and find themes or cause/effect relationships. Share the method with your team, creating a culture that encourages people to probe for underlying issues.

Check your assumptions—Ask yourself and others what the underlying assumptions are for a given position, opinion, or preference. If you're taking a stance on an issue, why? If your perspective differs from others', ask them to "sell" the solution they favor. What are their underlying assumptions or intentions? Help people see embedded biases and encourage others to do the same for you. Challenge yourself and others to advocate for someone else's idea; look for the value in others' points of view and ideas. Conversely, have someone play the role of critic, even for ideas that seem obvious or promising.

Create a criteria check sheet—First, determine a set of criteria for your pending decision. What are the requirements? What does the decision need to accomplish? What constraints exist? Once you have a list of criteria, prioritize items and evaluate each potential solution against the criteria. Consider using a decision matrix, by which you rate each option against the criteria using a 4-point scale: How likely is it that the decision will meet the criteria? (1) Very unlikely, (2) Somewhat unlikely, (3) Somewhat likely, (4) Very likely, or (U) Unsure. For "Unsure" responses, think about investigating further, especially if the criterion is a higher priority. For many "unlikely" ratings, try generating more solutions.

8

Create a "project plan" for an important decision—Working backward from when the decision needs to be made, schedule the start and end time and identify the resources needed for each key step in the process. It's not always a linear process. You might get to the generating alternatives phase and decide to go back and seek more information. Still, having a plan with specific steps and milestones as well as timelines will help you make the decision in the allotted time frame. If the decision is delayed, review your plan to identify where and why. What was the impact of the delay? How can you avoid similar obstacles in the future?

Communicate progress and actions—Following the full decision-making process can take time. Keep stakeholders informed and engaged. Set weekly or monthly reminders to send updates. If the decision hasn't progressed, key stakeholders will want to know, and they might be able to assist with obstacles.

Time it right—Scientists suggest that timing your brainstorming and decision-making efforts with your high energy level and mental sharpness can make a big difference. Plan early brainstorming sessions because people are least creative when it's demanded most: at the heart of the workday, between 11 a.m. and 3 p.m. People also tend to make the worst decisions late at night and first thing in the morning. Your cognitive skills are strongest once your brain has shaken off sleep inertia, so make important decisions when you feel most alert—generally within one to three hours after waking up.

8 ▶▶▶ Stretch It... Apply your decision-making skills in more challenging ways.

Reflect on past decisions—Set reminders to reflect on key decisions at various points (e.g., a week, month, quarter, or year afterward). Examine what went right or wrong after the decision was implemented. Were there unanticipated consequences? Were some stakeholders affected but not involved? Did overlooked data surface later? Consider what you can do better the next time. Similarly, compare one of your best decisions to one of your worst. What was different or the same? Decide what you will and won't do the next time.

Understand your organization's strategic goals—Even for day-to-day or operational decisions, you can craft better criteria and evaluate options if you understand your organization's strategic direction. Find out how your team's functions contribute to organizational objectives. What are those objectives, and how are they measured and reported? Consider joining meetings with senior leaders.

Review shareholder or earnings reports. Ask a veteran manager about previous high-impact decisions in your organization. Which ones benefited a team or department but had negative organizational consequences, and vice versa? Discuss successes, failures, and the decision-making process used. Consider what actions you can take or decisions you can make to better align your team and the organization.

Look for an organizational partner who models effective decision making—Is there an internal partner (perhaps a leader in another department) who consistently involves you or your team in decisions or seeks your input on shared processes? What can you observe about this person's style? Also consider accompanying an experienced salesperson on a customer call. How does the person gather quantitative and qualitative information from the customer to develop a sales strategy and find the right solution?

Track recurring problems—Often your smaller-scope, daily decisions aren't memorable. What requests do you get or problems do you see so often they're considered routine? Track the problem, date, time of occurrence, and related stakeholders. Assess your list after two weeks and identify recurring issues. Is there a clear process or personnel concern? A budget or communication issue? Also reflect on common topics in meetings and informal discussions. Which come up frequently? What are your team members complaining about or what issues never seem to be fully resolved? Look for themes, trends, and relationships among them. Is there a process or person in common? Can you find a root cause?

Decide in a different context—Look for community organizations in which you can serve in a decision-making capacity. Volunteer to serve on a project that is analyzing a problem or opportunity. Joining a new group often forces you to gather and interpret information—steps you might otherwise replace with assumptions and status-quo ideas because you're overly familiar. Try this internally, too. Ask your manager for special assignments—such as leading a cross-functional team—requiring decision making in less-familiar situations.

Review case studies—Business cases summarize fictitious or real-life events faced by management, companies, and industries. Some publishers produce and sell cases for learning purposes; other sources include books, articles, and free Internet sites. Case studies provide a framework for problem solving. You can analyze situations in which you lack first-hand experience and practice critical thinking and problem-solving skills.

8

Support for developing Decision Making

Adaptability. You might feel confident about a decision you've made, but what if it looks like you won't get the results you expected? Don't let your conviction or persistence become unproductive; be willing to quickly change course. Revisit alternatives you considered previously and be ready to implement a contingency plan.

Continuous Learning. The best problem solvers are often intellectually curious, so broaden your knowledge base. While many of your decisions are likely based on deep knowledge of your role, functional area, or industry, try putting yourself in unfamiliar situations so you can learn and ask questions. Take on challenging assignments where you're not an expert. By expanding your awareness and understanding, you become better equipped to analyze and interpret information. This improved understanding can lead you to generate more enlightened and creative solutions.

Driving for Results. Many leaders are overly cautious. They fully analyze the problem and select the best possible solution, yet hesitate to make the decision. Or they vacillate among solutions for too long. Your analysis of a problem should include determining the priority of the issue and the consequences of delayed action. Bring the appropriate sense of urgency to critical decisions. Expedite parts of the decision-making process if needed, and don't let any one part of the process drag on. Are you juggling many decision-making opportunities? Use a tracking system to monitor progress and avoid distractions.

8

9 Delegation and Empowerment

Sharing tasks and decision-making responsibilities to increase others' commitment, accelerate results, and build capability.

The Spirit of This Competency

How often do you try to do everything yourself because you think no one can do it as well as you? To succeed as a leader, you need to let go. Try sharing responsibilities with your direct reports, peers, and partners in a way that builds their capabilities and empowers them. If that makes you a little nervous, you can delegate more confidently if you clarify expectations, create ownership, and provide support. Otherwise, you'll soon burn out as you try to handle everything yourself, and—even worse—you'll miss opportunities to energize and engage others.

Self-Insight Questions

How are you doing at Delegation and Empowerment right now? Ask yourself:

- What's keeping me from sharing more work or responsibilities with others?

- When I delegate, do I choose the most appropriate person or team for the task?

- Do I just delegate tasks, or do I empower people by sharing more authority and responsibility?

- How could I encourage people to take more ownership of assigned tasks and responsibilities?

- How effectively do I provide guidance and support after I delegate a task or empower someone?

Key Actions: Building Blocks for Success

Key Actions are behaviors that work together to help you demonstrate this competency effectively.

Identify opportunities to share responsibility—Assign decision-making or task responsibility to people based on their abilities, availability, motivation, and development needs.

Clarify performance expectations—Communicate the importance and parameters of the delegation, including scope, decision-making authority, performance standards, and expected outputs and their impact. Explore the person's or team's issues and concerns.

9

Provide support without removing task ownership—Suggest resources and provide coaching. Offer timely feedback so people continue performance that's effective and improve less-effective work or results. Express confidence in people.

Involve others in agreements—Generate commitment by asking for the other person's ideas when agreeing on performance expectations, support needed, how results will be measured, and follow-up actions.

Stay informed—Establish ways you can stay aware of issues, follow up on action items, and track results.

When you're delegating and empowering effectively, you'll notice:

Your team displays more initiative, and people are increasing their capabilities.

- People are developing. They feel empowered to take on more responsibility, accept new roles, and build their skills. They're more satisfied with their work.
- Your team's capacity is growing. Team members accomplish goals they were unable to achieve before and have higher productivity without additions to staff.
- People feel a greater sense of ownership. They drive their own performance results.
- Your staff sees your delegations as opportunities, not just more work for them. People are eager to assume more decision-making authority as the assignment progresses.
- An empowered team seeks your input—but not always your decision. They think of potential solutions and recommendations before they involve you.
- Other parts of the organization see your team as highly skilled and productive.

You have more time available to accomplish your goals.

- You spend less time dealing with day-to-day issues and can focus on leading your team and achieving strategic priorities.
- Your team uncovers issues and resolves them before you notice they exist. You hear about minor problems after the team has solved them.
- You feel less stressed.
- You're confident in your team's ability to handle things when you're not there.

The team is focused and contributing to critical business priorities.

- Your team members have role clarity: They know what they need to do and have the skills to do it.
- Team members feel empowered and personally accountable for their goals. They understand the importance of their contributions to larger team goals and organizational success.
- You use delegation and empowerment as part of a growth strategy, with an eye toward developing talent while accomplishing current business priorities.

9

Critical Leadership Moments

As a leader, you face situations, or **Critical Leadership Moments,** that stretch your skills. Delegation and Empowerment can help you to:

Engage

▸ Empower Your Team

▸ Prepare Someone for an Ambitious Assignment

Drive

▸ Share More Responsibility with Your Team

▸ Hold Team Members Accountable for Delivering Results

▸ Execute a Major Project or Business Initiative

Delegation and Empowerment is **essential** for success if you want to:

Empower Your Team

To build team commitment by offering meaningful work and motivational guidance, focus on these **Key Actions:**

- **Identify opportunities to share responsibility** and challenge people to take on new and interesting assignments.
- **Provide support without removing task ownership** by offering resources, feedback, and coaching as you build the person's independence and confidence.
- **Involve others in agreements** to build their commitment to action.

Also see the **Coaching** competency to be even better prepared for this Critical Leadership Moment.

Share More Responsibility with Your Team

To confidently delegate important tasks to team members more often, focus on these **Key Actions:**

- **Identify opportunities to share responsibility** by looking for new assignments in which to empower others with more decision-making authority.
- **Clarify performance expectations** to define responsibility for assignments and set boundaries for decision making.
- **Stay informed** to ensure the person's success and increase your comfort with letting go. Follow up to uncover issues early, confirm people have taken action, and track results.

Also see the **Guiding Team Success** competency to be even better prepared for this Critical Leadership Moment.

9

Hold Team Members Accountable for Delivering Results

To ensure employees are clear about their responsibilities and expectations for delivering results, focus on these **Key Actions:**

- **Clarify performance expectations** to ensure accountabilities and outcomes are clearly defined.
- **Involve others in agreements** to gain their buy-in to goals, outcome measures, and follow-up actions.
- **Stay informed** by following up on action items, asking about concerns, and tracking results.

Also see the **Execution** competency to be even better prepared for this Critical Leadership Moment.

 ## Delegation and Empowerment will **boost** your success if you want to:

Prepare Someone for an Ambitious Assignment

While **Coaching** is essential for helping team members and colleagues face a new challenge, delegating frequently and purposefully will build people's skills and prepare them for more ambitious assignments.

Execute a Major Project or Business Initiative

While **Execution** is essential for ensuring the success of a project, delegating the right responsibilities to the right person or team helps to ensure projects move along at the proper pace and people meet critical milestones and deadlines.

9

⚠ Common Mistakes

You can avoid common Delegation and Empowerment errors by paying attention to how people react to your efforts.

Under Actions

When you don't demonstrate the Key Actions for Delegation and Empowerment effectively, the results can be disappointing.

If you notice that:	You might be:	Try these quick remedies:
Your team lacks motivation and direction	**Dumping, not delegating**	• Choose assignments that fit the other person's skills and motivations. Avoid unloading unpleasant tasks in the name of "empowerment." • Set people up for success by making sure they have the resources and skills to carry out the task. Delegating doesn't relieve you of responsibility for results. • Clarify roles and define the boundaries of people's authority. Uncertainty often leads people to be indecisive.
People aren't accepting accountability	**Allowing tasks to boomerang to you**	• Clearly communicate that the person is responsible for completing the task. • Offer guidance when a person comes to you for help, but don't take back responsibility for tasks. Reverse delegation blurs the boundaries of accountability. • Provide feedback and coaching that move people toward more self-directed decision making.
You don't trust others enough to delegate to them	**Trying to do everything yourself**	• Delegate even when you feel uncomfortable. Choose less-critical tasks at first, then share more responsibilities as you build confidence in others' abilities. • Challenge high-potential team members by delegating stretch assignments so that the best people are being developed. Help them see the value of their contributions and commitment.
People take too long to finish their delegated tasks	**Neglecting to check in and follow up**	• Empowerment can add to a person's workload. Be patient and offer support to help people grow into new roles and responsibilities. • Conduct progress reviews often and then offer the right level of coaching.

Over Actions

When you demonstrate certain Delegation and Empowerment Key Actions at an extreme level, it can lead to poor results.

If you notice that:	You might be:	Try these quick remedies:
The workload isn't balanced across team members	**Delegating to one person too often**	• Balance work across individuals based on their capabilities, motivation, and availability. Avoid delegating exclusively to one particularly competent person. • Ask yourself why you always delegate to the same person. Are you unconsciously biased in that person's favor, while depriving others of the opportunity to grow? Distribute delegations evenly to avoid demotivating people and discouraging their initiative.
People are resisting your follow-up	**Monitoring progress too closely**	• Build follow-up into your delegations, be available to team members at their discretion, and give them the authority needed to complete the assignment. • Avoid checking progress too often. This can feel intrusive and become counterproductive if it undermines confidence, motivation, and creativity.
People are hesitant to ask for help	**Expressing too much confidence**	• Moderate your displays of confidence by also letting people know that they can come to you for help. Showing too much confidence might discourage legitimate requests for guidance. Listen carefully for hints that the person needs and wants coaching.
Your team is too dependent on you	**Offering too much advice and support**	• Maintain a balance of support, resources, and guidance to inspire confidence and keep people on track without taking away their ownership. Empower people to become self-sufficient. Otherwise, they won't develop personal commitment or accountability. • Describe the desired outcome of the delegated task without telling the person how to do it. Offer support as needed. Providing too much advice can demotivate people, damage their self-confidence, and deprive them of satisfaction in their work.

9

Development Activities

Some of these activities will help you quickly address Critical Leadership Moments. Others require a greater investment of time and resources and can be part of your longer-term development plan. Choose the activities that work best for your goals.

▶▷▷ Prepare for It... Prepare for delegation and empowerment opportunities.

Change your mind-set—This competency is about letting go—sharing your decision-making power with your team to enable them to achieve their potential. That means encouraging others to assume greater responsibility while you exercise the discipline to back off and let them take the initiative and the risks—and make mistakes. You might find delegation challenging, but you'll soon view it as an essential leadership skill.

Establish a process to track distribution of work—Create a log of past and planned delegations to help you identify team members who have the time, motivation, and skills to take on new projects. When new responsibilities arise, use this tool to carefully match the individual to the requirements for success. Also, consider these assignments as opportunities for people to build their commitment and develop new capabilities, so the most experienced person might not always be the right choice. Meet with your team periodically to update the log and ensure you're not giving your best players too much work because they're so competent.

Analyze your workload and responsibilities—Identify tasks you could delegate. Classify each one based on the amount of authority you want to share:

- **Keep the task**—You need to hold onto both the authority and responsibility for handling the task.

- **Delegate idea generation**—You're ready to assign responsibility for coming up with ideas or solutions.

- **Delegate the task**—You want to assign responsibility for completing a well-defined task that involves little or no decision-making authority.

- **Delegate the authority**—You want to assign responsibility for completing a well-defined task that includes defined decision-making authority.

Strategize your delegations to achieve longer-term goals—Don't delegate just to get something done faster. Use delegation to ensure that every member of your team is contributing to important results and continually developing new expertise. Ask yourself how each assignment will build skills or move decision making closer to those who know the work best. At the same time, delegate to unlock your time and focus so you can tackle more strategic issues.

Create a development needs analysis—Examine team members' project histories and current skills. Use the analysis to identify individual development needs, then scan the landscape to provide people with challenging, visible, critical, and skill-enhancing assignments. Track their progress.

Create a delegation plan—Once you've identified a task or role and determined the right person, create a delegation plan. Include the importance of the assignment, who should be involved, a clear definition of the output expected, the time frame for completion, and the support you will provide. Meet with the person to share the plan.

▶▶▷ **Try It...** Practice your delegation and empowerment skills.

Create a safe delegation environment—If you're encouraging team members to work on challenging assignments and take risks, then be clear that making mistakes is part of the learning process and won't be punished—and then live up to that promise. Keep offering your support without removing their responsibility for the task. When people voice concerns, listen for their emotions and, through words and actions, show that you understand; don't dismiss or ignore their feelings.

Meet with people at the beginning of a delegation—Explain how individual responsibilities relate to the success of the team and organization. Communicate the parameters of the delegated responsibility, including scope and decision-making authority, due dates, expected outcomes, and their impact. Ask what resources are needed and agree on the support available. Ask the person to recommend an approach and work together to determine the best path, while exploring any issues and concerns.

Ask open-ended questions to involve people—Generate commitment by asking for people's ideas for executing the assignment, measuring results, and resolving issues. Show respect and appreciation for their contributions, regardless of their roles. Listen attentively to their questions—they might reveal concerns or doubts. Ask what coaching and support people need.

Agree on follow-up—Establish several interim deadlines over the course of the delegation so the person knows when specific tasks must be completed. Holding regular update meetings as well as informal talks (i.e., manage by walking around) will help ensure the person is meeting goals. Answer questions and provide guidance when requested, but otherwise stay out of the way so people can fully "own" the work. Provide timely constructive feedback on individual performance and recognize contributions and results along the way.

Assess your effectiveness at delegating—Hold a debriefing to review the results. Schedule follow-up meetings with key stakeholders to determine their satisfaction with results of a delegation. Peers and direct reports can offer useful feedback about the clarity of your delegations, helpfulness of the resources and support you provided, and the effectiveness of your follow-up. Ask people to identify any barriers they encountered, and then ask how you could eliminate them. Apply the insights you gain to improve your next delegation.

Identify projects in which more effective delegation might have led to a better outcome—For each situation, evaluate your effectiveness against this competency's Key Actions (i.e., Identify opportunities, Clarify performance expectations, Provide support, Involve others, Stay informed), so you know which behaviors you'll continue, do more often, or stop doing.

>>> **Stretch It...** Apply your delegation and empowerment skills in more challenging ways.

Empower and delegate even when it's most difficult—Think of something that you don't trust anyone but you to do—and then delegate it. Begin with low-risk decisions and work your way up to higher-risk issues. The more important the decision or task, the more uncomfortable it will feel to let go. When you face increased pressure for results and more complex issues, you might feel tempted to take back some control. Resist this urge as you set an example for others. People will commit to greater accountability if they see that you're sincere about relinquishing control.

9

Volunteer to lead a project team—Look for project management opportunities where you have no formal authority and team members have most of the responsibility for doing the work. Practice delegation and empowerment to assign tasks to the right people, build ownership, and get the work done on time.

Encourage team members to volunteer for roles that will stretch their skills—Suggest roles on important task forces or project teams that will increase team members' visibility and networking opportunities. If you normally participate in these activities, recommend team members to take these roles instead.

Develop a cross-training or job-rotation program within your team or area—Give people a chance to broaden their skills and explore other opportunities within their team or across teams. Team members could list the unique skills and knowledge they can share as well as which development needs they'd like to address through new assignments.

Lead a community, charitable, or political organization project—Look for roles outside work where you'll need to organize activities that involve complex tasks and will provide challenging delegation opportunities.

Support for developing Delegation and Empowerment

Emotional Intelligence Essentials. To truly empower others, you'll need to show confidence in their abilities. Be sure to maintain people's self-esteem, even when they make mistakes. Allow them the freedom to suggest ideas and tackle assignments using their own approaches.

Adaptability. Delegating a task often depends on your willingness to hand off responsibility and, to some extent, control. This can be uncomfortable because you are ultimately responsible for the outcomes. Adjust your mind-set; consider delegations as opportunities for others to learn and grow, and be open to the new, different, and possibly better ways someone else might handle the task.

Driving for Results. Delegation is often the best way to get things get done. To inspire others to achieve exceptional results, it's critical to agree on stretch goals; however, make sure to offer support and be available to help them overcome obstacles. You might sometimes lose track of the assignment—and so can the person carrying it out. Help the person stay focused by preventing distractions and continuously monitoring progress.

9

10 Driving Innovation

Sharing tasks and decision-making responsibilities to increase others' commitment, accelerate results, and build capability.

The Spirit of This Competency

Innovation is no longer a differentiator between more- and less-successful leaders and organizations. It's a requirement for survival. Fortunately, you don't need to come up with all the innovative ideas yourself. Instead, create an environment that inspires your team to generate novel solutions and experiment with unique ways to solve problems. Provide opportunities and tools for brainstorming to encourage them to come up with ideas. Then, empower team members with decision-making authority and resources so they can transform their most promising designs into real solutions.

Self-Insight Questions

How are you doing at Driving Innovation right now? Ask yourself:

- Do I encourage people to ask provocative questions that challenge current practices?

- How do I help people explore alternative ways to solve problems and achieve results?

- Would my team members say they feel safe to experiment, make mistakes, and fail?

- How often do I advocate for others' ideas to higher levels of management?

Key Actions: Building Blocks for Success

Key Actions are behaviors that work together to help you demonstrate this competency effectively.

Inspire curiosity—Encourage people to ask thought-provoking questions to understand stakeholders' needs and the rationale supporting current practices.

Challenge current thinking—Urge people to explore alternative ways to solve problems and achieve results; encourage idea generation; seek inspiration from diverse sources.

Support experimentation—Give people leeway to test promising ideas and empower them to take risks; reward attempts at innovation, whether successful or not.

10

Advance ideas to the next stage—Assertively advocate for others' ideas to management to secure the resources needed for successful implementation.

When you're driving innovation effectively, you'll notice:

Your team challenges the way things are currently done.

- People are curious and ask provocative questions to understand the rationale for current practices.
- People aren't satisfied with the answer "We've always done it this way." They want to know why.
- It's common for team members to question long-held assumptions and encourage others to look at problems from new perspectives.

People generate new solutions that better meet stakeholder (internal or external) needs.

- Your team strives to understand stakeholders' needs, concerns, and desires before suggesting solutions.
- When the team is evaluating new ideas, the top consideration is the impact on stakeholders (e.g., internal partners, suppliers, and customers).

People propose process enhancements that significantly improve quality, productivity, or efficiency.

- People propose ideas that have value and make a significant difference to results.
- People are willing to experiment with new processes and technology, even when they have reservations.
- You ensure that promising ideas are implemented successfully by securing the commitment, time, and resources needed.

10

Critical Leadership Moments

As a leader, you face situations, or **Critical Leadership Moments,** that stretch your skills. Driving Innovation can help you to:

Engage

▶ Encourage Experimentation and New Ideas

Manage

▶ Find the Best Solution Despite Limited Information

▶ Identify New Business Directions

Drive

▶ Get Results from Innovation Efforts

Driving Innovation is **essential** for success if you want to:

Encourage Experimentation and New Ideas

To create an environment in which people have the confidence to question and improve processes and solutions, focus on these **Key Actions:**

- **Inspire curiosity** by encouraging people to ask provocative questions that uncover stakeholder needs and challenge current practices.
- **Challenge current thinking** by urging people to explore alternative approaches to solving problems and coming up with ideas.
- **Support experimentation** by empowering people to test new ideas. Reward them for taking risks, whether the idea is or isn't successful.

Also see the **Facilitating Change** competency to be even better prepared for this Critical Leadership Moment.

10

Get Results from Innovation Efforts

To implement new ideas and solutions with discipline, even when innovation brings uncertainty, focus on these **Key Actions:**

- **Inspire curiosity** so others discover the full range of stakeholders' needs and to make sure their solutions achieve the desired results.
- **Support experimentation** by empowering people to test new ideas and then rewarding them for taking risks.
- **Advance ideas to the next stage** by advocating for them to management and securing the resources needed to make them a reality.

Also see the **Execution** competency to be even better prepared for this Critical Leadership Moment.

Driving Innovation will **boost** your success if you want to:

Find the Best Solution Despite Limited Information

While **Decision Making** is essential for problem solving when information is incomplete, creating a culture that encourages experimentation and risk taking helps the team feel secure enough to act, even with limited data.

Identify New Business Directions

While **Business Acumen** is essential for proposing strategic shifts based on industry and market knowledge, being curious and challenging established business models can yield bold, unique solutions that differentiate the business from competitors.

10

⚠ Common Mistakes

You can avoid common Driving Innovation errors by paying attention to how people react to your efforts.

Under Actions

When you don't demonstrate the Key Actions for Driving Innovation effectively, the results can be disappointing.

If you notice that:	You might be:	Try these quick remedies:
Only one solution is being considered	**Jumping to problem solving**	• Encourage your team to ask provocative questions that get at the rationale behind current practices and uncover stakeholders' needs before they move to the problem-solving phase. • Consider alternative perspectives and brainstorm multiple ideas to arrive at robust and innovative solutions, rather than rushing ahead with the first idea.
Your team lacks inspiration for new ideas	**Thinking "inside the box"**	• Bring innovation to your brainstorming process by suggesting a variety of tools and techniques to your team (see page 110 for examples). • Involve people with more diverse and cross-functional perspectives when developing solutions. More varied input leads to fewer decision-making errors and better quality solutions.
Your team avoids risky ideas	**Discouraging experimentation**	• Empower your team to make decisions and then reward their innovation attempts—even the unsuccessful ones. Show you value their involvement and ideas, not just the results. • Encourage your team to test promising ideas, push boundaries, and take risks with new technology.
New ideas never get implemented	**Neglecting execution**	• Assertively advocate for new ideas to higher management and help the team secure the time and resources needed to try out their best ideas. • After the team selects the best idea, start planning steps to execute it (e.g., creating accountability and timelines). • Identify individual, technological, or organizational barriers to implementing innovative ideas and gain support to eliminate them.

10

Over Actions

When you demonstrate certain Driving Innovation Key Actions at an extreme level, it can lead to poor results.

If you notice that:	You might be:	Try these quick remedies:
Your team takes too long to propose new solutions	**Afflicted with analysis paralysis**	• Urge the team to balance the time spent asking questions and exploring stakeholders' needs with time spent brainstorming and evaluating solutions. • Quickly zero in on the solutions that provide the most value for stakeholders. Spending too much time evaluating a wide range of solutions can mean missed opportunities.
Your team is overwhelmed with innovations	**Encouraging too many ideas**	• Evaluate each solution for potential impact before you implement it. Change for the sake of change can create chaos, intensify problems, and make others wary of your ideas. • Avoid starting so many initiatives that you can't execute them.
New solutions don't make an impact	**Innovating for the sake of innovation**	• Advocate only for ideas with the best chance of succeeding. Consider risks versus benefits before you encourage people to experiment and before you escalate ideas to management for support. • Make sure your team's innovation efforts address important work issues or opportunities. Avoid supporting ideas just because they are innovative or use the latest technology. They should align with the organization's priorities, provide value for stakeholders, and improve processes or results.

10

Development Activities

Some of these activities will help you quickly address Critical Leadership Moments. Others require a greater investment of time and resources and can be part of your longer-term development plan. Choose the activities that work best for your goals.

>>> **Prepare for It...** Prepare for opportunities to drive innovation.

Expand your mind-set—Exposure to diverse perspectives can facilitate new ideas. Some sources of relevant trends and market opportunities are international business and industry websites, blogs, podcasts, and publications. Encourage your team find new sources of inspiration by exploring industries, regions, and fields outside their areas of expertise. Ask yourself: What new relationships could I initiate to expand my team's perspective? Are there opportunities to collaborate with areas of my organization that my team is less familiar with? Could I create external relationships with universities, research groups, or industry associations?

Build creative teams—Recruit team members with unique skill sets and perspectives that supplement those of your current team. Look for people whose behaviors align with the Key Actions of Driving Innovation. People will be more excited to innovate if the task aligns with their motivations and interests, and the environment is informal, nonhierarchical, interdisciplinary, playful, and demanding. Let people know what's in it for them: increased visibility, management support, and opportunities to develop new relationships and knowledge. Make sure you have substantial management support before you recruit people.

Focus your team's improvement efforts—Align your team's innovation efforts with the organization's business strategy, talent management initiatives, and culture. Which areas would benefit most from a new approach? Avoid areas that require big investments of time, money, or effort but might not produce a substantial return.

Prepare a business case—A common obstacle to innovation efforts is the failure to build a business case for your ideas. Before presenting an idea, be sure the goals, methods, and implementation are grounded in facts. The more evidence and data you have to support an initiative, the more likely it is to be implemented and sustained. Ensure your team's proposals show return on investment (ROI), value for the customer, and a strong grasp of the market.

10

>>> **Try It...** Practice your skills for driving innovation.

Create a safe innovation culture—Model showing curiosity, questioning assumptions, taking risks, and considering novel ideas. Ask your team if you're inadvertently discouraging ideas (for example, by not listening, criticizing ideas, or displaying one-upmanship), and work on eliminating those behaviors. Communicate confidence in peoples' insights and build on their ideas via positive feedback. Reward curiosity, not just productivity.

Learn from mistakes and failure—Be clear that innovation requires experimentation and mistakes are expected. After your team completes a risky project, ask what went well and what could have gone better without placing blame for unsuccessful results. Instead, focus on how to improve the approach so people feel comfortable continuing to take risks and experiment.

Include a variety of perspectives when developing solutions—Seek the perspectives of people familiar with the situation as well as those who aren't but might have a unique point of view. Ask people from different departments or disciplines how they address situations or problems similar to yours.

Leverage digital communication channels—Use social media and team collaboration tools to share knowledge and ideas within and across teams. Besides gaining ideas from diverse perspectives, you can explore the impact of new solutions on other parts of the organization. Publicize experiments and lessons learned, ask for implementation ideas, and, of course, celebrate innovation successes by sharing them online.

Schedule "creativity time"—Write a problem statement and suggest that team members set aside quiet time to generate solutions and improvements individually. Then, as a group analyze and discuss the underlying causes of the problem. Brainstorm a number of possible solutions to address the underlying issues. Avoid judging the ideas while you're brainstorming. Then, evaluate each based on impact/effort or ease/expense of execution. Discuss several approaches (for example, aggressive versus conservative) before selecting the best strategy.

10

Challenge assumptions and encourage questions—Don't assume the current way is the best way to get something done. Ask your team to share assumptions about stakeholders (partners, customers, team members, etc.) and processes. Discuss the origins of the assumptions and decide how to test their validity. Separate facts from opinions and emotions from logic, and then explore alternative perspectives. Challenge yourself and others to constantly ask provocative, open-ended questions about the status quo, such as: "Why?" "Why not?" and "What if?"

Experiment with techniques for generating ideas—Here are some examples:

- **Storyboards** are a series of images and text shown in a sequence of steps. Once you have an idea, use storyboards to begin shaping the user experience. They can also convey the value of a solution to key stakeholders, explain proposed functionality to a colleague, or elicit feedback from stakeholders and users.

- **Concept mapping** helps the team organize and visualize ideas and discover the connections between them. Start with a focus question, then list the concepts (nouns), and, finally, link the concepts with verbs to describe their relationships.

- **Affinity clustering** helps to sort large amounts of information around a topic into logical groups based on similarities between items. Start by having team members write one item of interest per note, and with a stack of notes, work as a group to assemble categories. Identify the patterns that emerge, enabling teams to prioritize and plan next steps.

- **Problem tree analysis** can help the team discover links between causes and effects for a recurring problem. Draw one tree per problem. Repeatedly ask "why" to identify causes, and then link these to the main problem. Team members' discussion around this process becomes its true value as they uncover the root cause of problems.

- **Thumbnail sketching** is a great way to use small drawings to explore, share, and build on many ideas quickly. Give yourself and your team a challenge and a time constraint. Then generate thumbnail sketches to develop the solution. Do a few rounds to refine the ideas; remember, they're just sketches, so encourage your team to churn out as many ideas as possible and throw out the bad ones without regret.

Recognize and reward innovation efforts—Set up formal and informal ways to reward team members' contributions to innovation goals. Reward thinking outside normal systems, processes, and procedures, even if a venture fails. To boost future engagement, plan an award ceremony to showcase innovative achievements to the broader organization.

Secure top management support—It's your job to make sure your team's ideas are well received and have a good chance of being executed. Find funding, space, and staffing to permit the group to fully pursue an idea. Push beyond concerns about short-term profit or return on net assets during initial phases of development. Help stakeholders see the long-term payoffs to garner their backing. A senior-level champion can help you gain support among the broader organization. This person can also be a sounding board as you refine your ideas and execution plan.

>>> **Stretch It...** Apply your driving innovation skills in more challenging ways.

Explore and anticipate customer needs—Find ways to expose your team to your customers' perspective: Give them opportunities to observe and interact with internal and external customers and other organizations in your industry. You might invite customers to speak at team meetings about their current business focus, or interview or survey customers to better understand their views on an upcoming change and how to make it a positive experience. Talk to former customers to find out why they no longer use your products or services. Encourage your team to identify customers' needs your organization currently doesn't meet and then brainstorm ways to expand products and services.

Create a stakeholder map—This map helps your team visualize and understand the interactions among all the people who will touch the product/service from purchase decision through use and maintenance. First, make a broad list of stakeholders, and draw icons to represent each person. Label individuals by specific role and write a speech bubble to summarize their thoughts and feelings about their needs and priorities. Draw arrows to connect people and label the arrows to describe relationships. With this understanding, brainstorm activities you can add, refine, or eliminate to better meet stakeholder needs.

Sponsor innovation competitions—Explore a problem and generate new solutions by establishing a formal innovation process within your culture. Link the problem statement to a strategic outcome and define the requirements of the submission. Reinforce the process by recognizing all submissions, and act on the top choices.

Test one of your team's riskier ideas—Choose a noncritical situation and encourage your team to test one of its riskier ideas. Ask colleagues to evaluate your team's plan for implementing the idea and to challenge every aspect of it, pointing out possible problems. Choose evaluators with varying levels of expertise to get the most valuable feedback. Adjust your plan based on what you learn.

10

Sponsor a "lunch and learn"—Meet once a month with your team to explore emerging business or industry trends and connect them to problems and opportunities the team is working on. Announce a single topic in advance and include prep work, such as reading an article or watching a video. Ask people to take turns leading the discussion.

Support for developing Driving Innovation

Adaptability. You're more likely to encourage innovation in others if you're open to change. Show others that you're ready to experiment with new approaches and willing to accept solutions that transform the way work gets done.

Continuous Learning. Learn about areas outside your expertise. As you gain knowledge and experience, you'll think about problems and opportunities from a new perspective, and that can lead to new solutions.

Driving for Results. Innovation requires more than novel thinking. Focus the team only on ideas that meet important customer (internal or external) needs and improve high-priority business results. To help the team succeed, set stretch goals, ensure accountabilities, and support them in overcoming obstacles.

10

11 Emotional Intelligence Essentials

Developing trusting relationships by effectively interpreting and responding to your and others' emotions.

The Spirit of This Competency

The emotional impact of what you say and do gives you the power to inspire trust and enthusiasm or—on the other hand—promote antagonism and resistance. Of all the competencies vital to great leadership, Emotional Intelligence Essentials is likely the most undervalued and, thus, underused. What could be more important than increasing your insight into your and others' emotions and then managing the situation to achieve the results that you want? Once you understand how your reactions support or undermine your impact, you can respond in ways that help you connect with and energize other people. You'll create a work environment in which trust, collaboration, and empowerment thrive.

Self-Insight Questions

How are you doing with demonstrating Emotional Intelligence Essentials right now? Ask yourself:

- Do I understand my emotional triggers? How could I adjust my reactions to improve my impact?

- How often do I ask for others' opinions and ideas? Do I show that I value their contributions?

- How well do I maintain others' self-esteem when things don't go well?

- How often do I respond with empathy when others express their concerns?

- How could I lead discussions better?

Key Actions: Building Blocks for Success

Key Actions are behaviors that work together to help you demonstrate this competency effectively.

Build self-awareness—Understand your emotional triggers, strengths, and development needs as well as the impact of your behavior on others.

Maintain self-control—Modify your behavior based on self-awareness to improve your impact and build relationships.

Maintain or enhance self-esteem—Acknowledge others' ideas, contributions, and achievements. Offer positive feedback. Focus on facts and intentions when things don't go well.

Listen and respond with empathy—Show that you understand the other person's situation by acknowledging both the facts and the feelings (positive or negative) he or she is expressing.

Ask for help and encourage involvement—Ask for others' opinions and ideas to enhance collaboration, encourage responsibility, and gain commitment.

Share thoughts, feelings, and rationale—Appropriately and honestly disclose your ideas, feelings, rationale, and insights to build trust.

Provide support without removing responsibility—Offer your help while building the other person's accountability and confidence.

Facilitate discussions—Conduct productive discussions by clarifying the situation, discussing ideas, and agreeing on next steps (use the Interaction Guidelines).

11

When you're using Emotional Intelligence Essentials effectively, you'll notice:

You communicate and leverage your values and emotions.

- You share your passions in ways that inspire and mobilize people.
- You're aware of your feelings in stressful moments. You stay calm and respond in ways that facilitate rather than interfere with your relationships and goals.
- You speak and act in ways that are consistent with your values and principles.

You often invite and act on feedback to improve.

- You have coworkers and leaders who give you honest feedback that helps you understand and correct your blind spots.
- You use insights from feedback to adjust your behavior and to improve your relationships.
- You can admit your weaknesses without being defensive.

Your interactions are collaborative, productive, and enjoyable.

- You listen more than you talk; you ask more than you tell.
- You focus on shared goals, encourage discussion, and respect opposing opinions.
- You can anticipate and handle emotionally sensitive situations effectively.
- People share their honest concerns and emotions with you.
- In discussions, everyone takes responsibility for achieving goals and taking follow-up action.

11

Why Is Emotional Intelligence Essentials So Important?

Critical Leadership Moments

The Critical Leadership Moments Directory in Chapter 2 lists the competencies that are most important for success for each situation. However, you won't see Emotional Intelligence Essentials linked to any Critical Leadership Moment because this competency enhances your performance in almost every situation. Consider Emotional Intelligence Essentials a foundational skill for making all your interactions more effective.

Emotional Intelligence Essentials Supports Your Development in Other Competencies

Emotional Intelligence Essentials helps you build trusting relationships by increasing your self-awareness and your sensitivity to others' emotions. In this way, it helps your performance in most of the other competencies. DDI's research shows that most leaders fail not because they lack knowledge or technical skill, but due to interpersonal and communication shortcomings. These fundamental interaction skills keep people engaged, satisfied, motivated, and productive.

You can think of Emotional Intelligence Essentials as a "supercompetency" because it includes behaviors that are building blocks for outstanding performance in many other competencies. For example, the Key Action "listen and respond with empathy" is especially important in competencies, such as Coaching, Facilitating Change, and Influencing, that require you to soften others' resistance. Even competencies such as Decision Making and Delegation and Empowerment include behaviors that motivate people to share their ideas and commit to action ("ask for help and encourage involvement").

Interaction Essentials℠: The Keys to Communication Success

11

Most of the Emotional Intelligence Essentials Key actions are built on the Interaction Essentials℠. These skills help you lead productive discussions in a way that engages peoples' hearts and heads. **Key Principles** help you "lead with your heart" so you meet people's emotional needs. **Interaction Guidelines** help you "engage people's heads" so you meet practical needs and achieve business outcomes.

Key Principles

Emotional Intelligence Essentials includes five Key Actions you can take to help people feel valued, involved, and supported. They are known as the Key Principles:

Esteem—Maintain or enhance self-esteem.

Empathy—Listen and respond with empathy.

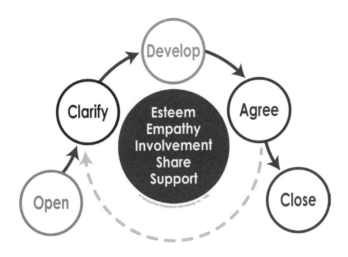

Involvement—Ask for help and encourage involvement.

Share—Share thoughts, feelings, and rationale.

Support—Provide support without removing responsibility.

The Key Principles form the foundation for many other competencies, especially those focused on interactions in which you're building relationships, influencing people, and gaining commitment to action. If you develop these core behaviors, you'll enhance your performance in other competencies at the same time.

Interaction Guidelines

The last Key Action in Emotional Intelligence Essentials, "facilitates discussions," includes a set of steps called Interaction Guidelines. You'll also find them in other competencies. Following these steps will make all your interactions more productive, whether you're leading large meetings, small team discussions, or one-on-one conversations:

Open—Describe the purpose and importance of the discussion.

Clarify—Seek and share information to clarify the situation, issues, and concerns.

Develop—Seek and discuss ideas. Explore needed resources and support.

Agree—Specify actions and confirm how to measure results.

Close—Highlight important features of the plan. Confirm confidence and commitment.

Note: At the end of every competency chapter is a section that explains how Emotional Intelligence Essentials supports your performance and development in that competency.

⚠ Common Mistakes

You can avoid common Emotional Intelligence Essentials errors by paying attention to how people react to your efforts.

Under Actions

When you don't demonstrate the Key Actions for Emotional Intelligence Essentials effectively, the results can be disappointing.

If you notice that:	You might be:	Try these quick remedies:
People keep their distance	**Lacking self-insight**	• When you feel strong emotions, pause to understand what you're feeling and why. Compose yourself, choose your response, and then look and listen for others' reactions. • After discussions, ask how the other person is feeling. You might be surprised. Can you change your behavior to improve your impact?
You're the last one to hear bad news	**Letting your emotions highjack your reactions**	• When things go wrong, do you lose emotional control? Such outbursts erode trust and cause people to withhold information. Identify your emotional triggers and then express your reactions more appropriately.
People don't confide in you	**Lacking empathy**	• When people express their emotions, empathize to show them you're listening. Ask questions to understand what they're going through. Open lines of communication, so they'll trust you with future confidences. • If you feel uncomfortable when someone reveals negative emotions, instead of focusing on your discomfort, acknowledge the facts of the situation and the emotions you observe. Don't jump to solve the problem—most people just want to be heard.
People are resistant or uncooperative	**Making others feel undervalued**	• It's easy to get so task focused that you forget to show others your appreciation. Take the time to acknowledge people's expertise, contributions, and achievements. • When giving feedback, reinforce others' efforts regardless of results. Focus on the facts and their good intentions when things don't go well to maintain their self-esteem.

11

Over Actions

When you demonstrate certain Emotional Intelligence Essentials Key Actions at an extreme level, it can lead to poor results.

If you notice that:	You might be:	Try these quick remedies:
People are too quiet during meetings and discussions	Shutting down participation	• Do you push others through your agenda without checking for their ideas and buy-in? Balance your agenda with others' needs. • Avoid presenting a problem and your plan to fix it. Instead, ask others to contribute to problem solving to increase their commitment to the solution.
Your positive feedback isn't having an impact	Too complimentary or understanding	• Offering indiscriminate compliments can seem insincere. Meaningful positive feedback is appropriate to the achievement and given selectively. • Communicate that you understand how someone is feeling without approving or excusing unacceptable behavior.
Conflicts are not being addressed	Avoiding emotionally charged situations	• Address conflict and barriers directly and honestly so you can solve them collaboratively. If you skirt sensitive issues, you'll decrease accountability. • Emotional intelligence is not about being "nice." In fact, you often have to confront difficult issues. Maintain people's self-esteem by sticking to the facts and assuming positive intentions.
Everything takes too long	Involving others too much	• You need to involve others to gain their commitment, but gathering input can slow progress. Be strategic about whom you involve and when. • Involving others can improve your decisions and solutions, but sometimes you need to go solo. If you can't reach consensus, proceed based on your best judgment.

11

Development Activities

Some of these activities will help you quickly address Critical Leadership Moments. Others require a greater investment of time and resources and can be part of your longer-term development plan. Choose the activities that work best for your goals.

▷▷▷ Prepare for It... Prepare for opportunities to demonstrate emotional intelligence.

Prepare for discussions—Plan the best interpersonal approach to help you reach your desired outcomes. Think through how you will:

- Explain the purpose and importance of the discussion.
- Clarify the situation by seeking and sharing information.
- Involve others and develop their ideas.
- Gain agreement on solutions.
- Close with a summary of conclusions and follow-up actions.

Anticipate disagreements—Before a discussion, identify the problems and goals you share with other participants. Focus on this common ground when trying to agree on solutions. Anticipate objections and other negative reactions. What will you say to empathize with and address concerns? How will you maintain people's self-esteem, especially in a heated discussion? How will you use self-disclosure to build trust?

Manage others' perceptions of you—Strive to make a good first impression. Understand your impact on others. Keep track of any incidents when others have mistaken your intentions. How could you alter your approach to avoid such misunderstandings?

Take on an emotionally intelligent mind-set—Only when you make an effort to be aware of your emotional reactions and consciously adjust them do you gain the power to change. Become aware of your emotional triggers; anticipate and control inappropriate reactions. Try not to take issues or disagreements personally; doing so can cloud your judgment, cause stress, and hinder progress. Approach situations from the other person's perspective. Ask him or her:

- How will this affect you?
- What do you think needs to happen to reach your goals?
- What can I do to help you meet your needs?

Attend workshops and webinars that build emotional intelligence skills—To be effective, the training should include topics such as enhancing self-awareness, practicing new skills in a safe environment, immediate feedback, and formal progress checks. Practice using skills in realistic situations to transfer the skills you learn in training to your work relationships.

11

▶▶▶ **Try It...** Practice emotional intelligence skills.

Create a supportive emotional environment—Good feelings spread more powerfully than bad, so share your emotions in an appropriate way. Help others do the same by encouraging honest, open discussions about both tasks and relationships. Show support by exploring concerns. Offer your time and expertise when you anticipate that others need help. Avoid taking credit for success and blaming others for failure. Stand up for people and back their ideas, decisions, and actions. Look for situations in which others' accomplishments or abilities are taken for granted. Acknowledge their contributions and advocate for recognition.

Continuously seek feedback—Periodically ask your manager, peers, direct reports, partners, and customers for feedback to find out their perceptions of your interpersonal effectiveness. Ask them how well you used each Key Principle. If you led a discussion, ask how well you followed the Interaction Guidelines. Make it clear that you're always open to feedback, including feedback for improvement. Remember, development is an ongoing growth process.

Involve people to build engagement and commitment—Explain why team members are valuable to a meeting or discussion. Ask open-ended questions and draw quiet participants into the discussion. As you listen to responses, pay attention to body language, tone of voice, and facial expressions. Are these cues consistent with their words? Ask people to share their perspectives, ideas, and recommendations for resolving issues, especially when they differ from yours. Express appreciation for others' ideas and try to use them in the solution. Treating others' contributions with respect, regardless of a person's formal role, will build trust and commitment.

Discover how others see you—Use a 360-degree feedback survey (or interview people) to gather feedback from your boss, peers, partners, and direct reports. Ask them for an honest critique of your interpersonal skills using the Key Actions for Emotional Intelligence Essentials. Discuss the results with your reviewers. Where do you agree, and what surprised you? Instead of being defensive, ask questions to better understand their perceptions of you. Compare how they see you with who you want to be. Reflect on how you can improve your impact.

11

>>> **Stretch It...** Apply your emotional intelligence skills in more challenging ways.

Learn best practices from expert leaders—Observe leaders who excel at building trusting relationships and who expertly manage their emotions and respond effectively to others' emotions. Compare your approach with theirs. Interview them to find out how their emotional intelligence skills help them and their teams achieve results. Ask for specific examples. How have they learned from their past mistakes? Note what resonates with you and then commit to trying—or improving—these behaviors.

Build new relationships—Volunteer as a sports team coach, lead a community service organization, or participate in local politics. At work, get involved with a project or task force that includes people from diverse interest groups, functions, or departments. Forming new relationships can increase your awareness of your blind spots and give you opportunities to experiment with new skills. In new relationships, people will have fewer preconceptions about your style, so you might find it easier to change some of your ingrained habits.

Help others improve how they're perceived—Help coworkers or direct reports see how their emotional impact enhances or interferes with their personal and team effectiveness. Be clear about any unacceptable behaviors and guide people in improving their responses and communication. Evaluate people's behavior objectively. Consider how they interact across various audiences and relationships. Don't stick with your first impression; base your perceptions on a variety of interactions.

Ask for help with a difficult situation—Ask someone who is strong in managing relationships to help you lead a meeting or discussion that you expect to be difficult. Notice what your co-leader does and says to navigate the sensitive points of the discussion. Join him or her in guiding the discussion toward productive outcomes. Ask your co-leader to observe you during the discussion and then give you examples of what you said and did that worked well. Also, discuss behavior changes that could enhance your effectiveness.

11

Support for developing Emotional Intelligence Essentials

Adaptability. A crucial component of Emotional Intelligence Essentials is adapting your behavior to make the most of your relationships. Awareness of your and others' emotions isn't enough; if you don't adjust what you say and do to meet others' emotional needs, no parties are likely to leave the interaction feeling understood, appreciated, and satisfied. As your work responsibilities, coworkers, bosses, and tools change, stay attuned to new emotional cues and needs. If you approach these changes as growth opportunities, you can try out new behaviors that will help you meet the emotional demands of any situation.

Continuous Learning. To develop the self-insight that leads to strong emotional intelligence, take active steps to learn more about yourself and the people with whom you interact. Seek feedback to improve your interpersonal approach. This means asking people to help you understand the impact you're having on them and then using this knowledge to identify your strengths and development needs. At the same time, take steps to learn more about your coworkers, partners, and managers. The better you understand their perspectives and needs, the more effectively you can empathize with their feelings, involve them, and support them.

11

12 Execution

Maximizing your team's contributions to strategic priorities by focusing team members on critical goals, ensuring accountability, and measuring progress.

The Spirit of This Competency

Are you managing a project, implementing a change, leading a management initiative, or trying to improve operational results? As the leader closest to people doing the work, you have the ultimate responsibility for execution. It's up to you to put the right actions in motion to transform these team goals into concrete outcomes. People need a leader who can provide clear direction, accountability, and processes that will fortify their efforts. This means setting up the team for success, focusing their energy, monitoring progress, and offering support. Clearly, it takes a complex set of skills (including project planning, talent management, and communication) to ensure that your team has an enduring, positive impact.

Self-Insight Questions

How are you doing at Execution right now? Ask yourself:

- What do I do to ensure that people focus on the most critical team and organization goals?

- How do I encourage people to contribute to team goals and be accountable for project results?

- What specific progress and outcome measures do I use to evaluate my team's success?

- How effectively do I track and communicate my team's progress and accomplishments?

Key Actions: Building Blocks for Success

Key Actions are behaviors that work together to help you demonstrate this competency effectively.

Maintain focus—Identify and emphasize critical priorities over daily distractions to make sure your team's time and energy align with important organizational goals.

Measure progress and outcomes—Identify objective and quantifiable progress (lead) and outcome (lag) measures. Track and broadcast progress and accomplishments.

Ensure accountability—Assign priorities and reinforce who is responsible for each progress measure. Make sure people understand the consequences of meeting or not meeting expectations. Identify measures that are on track and those that are at risk. Address any gaps in skill.

12

When you're executing effectively, you'll notice:

Your team's energy is focused on the team's and organization's priorities.

- People are clear about the team's and the organization's goals and understand their importance.

- People know their roles and accountabilities and how their work contributes to broader goals and strategies.

- Everyday activities and decisions align with project goals and higher-level priorities. The team avoids letting distractions take their time and focus.

- Your team accomplishes the highest-priority activities that contribute to the project's and the organization's results.

Your team's processes support the successful implementation of critical goals.

- Individuals' performance goals directly advance the team's (and organization's) priorities.

- People are compensated and rewarded for actions that contribute to important team (and organization) goals.

- Team communication processes encourage the free flow of information among team members and leaders.

- Measurement methods assess criteria that align with the desired outcomes of the project or initiative.

- Resources are allocated based on team and project priorities. The people with the right skills are assigned to the right responsibilities.

Your team clearly sees their impact on important results.

- The measurements you've put in place show that your team is accomplishing what it set out to do.

- Both quantitative and qualitative indicators show your team's impact on important goals and results. Metrics might focus on cost, quality, quantity, customer satisfaction, number of errors, safety incidents, or timeliness.

- People are motivated because they see progress toward achieving critical goals; they don't feel like the team is stagnant or stuck.

12

Critical Leadership Moments

As a leader, you face situations, or **Critical Leadership Moments,** that stretch your skills. Execution can help you to:

Drive

▶ Focus the Team on Critical Business Priorities

▶ Execute a Major Project or Business Initiative

▶ Provide Team Structure and Direction

▶ Hold Team Members Accountable for Delivering Results

▶ Make Change Happen

▶ Get Results from Innovation Efforts

  Execution is **essential** for success if you want to:

Focus the Team on Critical Business Priorities

To keep the team's efforts focused on the most important team and organizational goals, focus on these **Key Actions:**

- **Maintain focus** by steering your team toward the activities that contribute most to broader project and organization goals.

- **Measure progress and outcomes.** Track results using actionable measures. Identify any results that are at risk.

- **Ensure accountability** by making it clear: who's doing what, by when?. Make sure people have the skills they need to take on new responsibilities.

Also see the **Guiding Team Success** competency to be even better prepared for this Critical Leadership Moment.

Execute a Major Project or Business Initiative

To ensure that projects and initiatives are planned and have the resources needed for successful, on-time execution, focus on these **Key Actions:**

- **Maintain focus** by clarifying the most important project priorities and then steering the team's work toward those results. Redirect efforts if the team gets distracted with less-important issues or projects.

- **Measure progress and outcomes** with objective tracking methods. Keep your team and stakeholders informed of progress, setbacks, and results.

- **Ensure accountability** by assigning individual project responsibilities where people can best contribute their talents. Communicate the consequences of meeting or not meeting deadlines or achieving results. Address any gaps in skill.

Also see the **Delegation and Empowerment** competency to be even better prepared for this Critical Leadership Moment.

12

Execution will **boost** your success if you want to:

Provide Team Structure and Direction

While **Guiding Team Success** is essential for providing the team with the structure and guidance to accomplish key tasks, an execution plan will align your team's actions with broader project or organization goals.

Hold Team Members Accountable for Delivering Results

While **Delegation and Empowerment** is essential for ensuring that people are clear about their responsibilities for delivering individual results, your execution skills will ensure that your delegations align with broader team and business unit priorities.

Make Change Happen

While **Facilitating Change** is essential for getting your team through the challenges and disruptions of change, an execution plan will make sure roles, accountabilities, and processes support new ways of doing things.

Get Results from Innovation Efforts

While **Driving Innovation** is essential for generating and implementing new solutions, your execution skills provide the structure and the discipline to turn great ideas into reality with measurable results.

12

⚠ Common Mistakes

You can avoid common Execution errors by paying attention to how people react to your efforts.

Under Actions

When you don't demonstrate the Key Actions for Execution effectively, the results can be disappointing.

If you notice that:	You might be:	Try these quick remedies:
Your team is busy, but they're not advancing important goals	**Focusing on the wrong priorities**	• Align your team's activities with broader business priorities. • Refocus the team on the important, not the urgent, to keep the top priorities moving forward. Align your leadership decisions with those same priorities.
People aren't motivated to contribute to the organization's initiatives	**Failing to hold individuals accountable**	• Identify your team's goals; list each action and milestone. Clarify individual roles and responsibilities for each action. • Communicate clear performance expectations. Share the benefits of meeting—and the consequences of not meeting—expectations. Link performance evaluations and rewards to achieving those results. • Resolve duplication of effort and clarify who is accountable for what. People need to know what's expected of them to achieve results.
The team doesn't understand its impact on the organization's results	**Neglecting to track and communicate progress**	• Establish open communication channels so people see how their actions contribute to project success as well as the organization's broader results. • Define the criteria for a successful implementation. Establish lead and lag measures to track results. (Lead measures offer early indicators of success, whereas lag measures reveal the ultimate outcome.)
People aren't prepared to contribute to important goals	**Failing to anticipate resource needs**	• Prepare the people carrying out the execution plan for the unique demands of the project. Identify and close any gaps in skill. Ensure that communication, training, and resources are in place to support the project.

12

Over Actions

When you demonstrate certain Execution Key Actions at an extreme level, it can lead to poor results.

If you notice that:	You might be:	Try these quick remedies:
Projects get started but never completed	**Taking on too much**	• Avoid taking on more than you or your team can complete effectively. You need time and focus to prepare and execute thorough plans for each project. • Choose the projects or team initiatives that will have the most impact. A targeted approach will help you channel people's energy and hold them accountable for results.
Team performance isn't improving	**Overemphasizing tracking without taking corrective action**	• Tracking measures will reveal inefficiencies or loss of focus, so analyze the information often and adjust activities, timelines, or resources to get back on track. • Confront ineffective performance or unnecessary delays. Accepting poor results destroys accountability.
Team members are hesitant to act independently	**Micromanaging**	• Although it's tempting to step in frequently, balance providing direction with empowering others. Look for opportunities to delegate decisions and encourage your team to act without your direction. • Conduct regular check-ins with team members to make sure they understand their responsibilities and expectations. Reinforce accountability by commending people for accomplishments. Identify any areas that are off track and offer guidance.

12

Development Activities

Some of these activities will help you quickly address Critical Leadership Moments. Others require a greater investment of time and resources and can be part of your longer-term development plan. Choose the activities that work best for your goals.

▶▷▷ Prepare for It... Prepare for opportunities use your execution skills.

Learn more about your organization's strategies—The better you understand your organization's goals, the more credibly you can communicate these priorities and their implications to your team. Ask to attend meetings at higher levels where plans for executing business strategies will be discussed. Read internal resources that describe your organization's purpose, values, and strategies. Follow external sources to stay on top of industry, market, and competitive shifts. Even if some information isn't immediately relevant to your team, you'll be ready when senior leaders unveil the next organizational initiative. You'll confidently communicate the benefits and prepare your team to implement the new directive.

Make sure your team members know they're critical to the organization's success—Do your team members understand how their efforts affect the organization's results? Explain how strategic priorities cascading from senior levels to managers and then to individual contributors drive your team's priorities and performance expectations. Provide practical examples of how the organization's strategy and culture should guide individual and team priorities, decision making, and actions. Model these decisions and actions, and communicate your support for organization initiatives and directives; help your team understand the benefits. Be sensitive not to inadvertently discourage the team's confidence in strategic initiatives.

Align systems, processes, and capabilities—Identify the team processes that will have the most impact on achieving one of your team's priorities. Consider how each process or practice currently helps or hinders achieving this goal:

- Are training and development opportunities offered to build the skills and competencies needed to achieve the goal?
- Are people selected and promoted based on the skills and competencies required to achieve the goal?
- Are you an advocate of the priority? Do you model the values needed to keep others committed?
- Do information systems and team collaboration tools support reaching the goal?
- Do your performance and reward practices support the goal?

How will you make the best use of any supportive processes? How can you and your team change or minimize the impact of practices that don't align with your goals?

12

>>> **Try It...** Practice your execution skills.

Build an execution plan—Choose a project or team goal that you are responsible for achieving and create a plan. Ensure that your leaders support the plan and the people who will carry it out understand their roles in making the plan succeed.

- **Translate the team priority or project goals** into a plan with specific, measurable actions and accountabilities.
- **Identify each step** the team will take to reach the ultimate goal. These milestones help people see the path forward, identify points to measure progress, and figure out how each person can contribute.
- **Identify clear owners** for each action. Once you have established clear performance expectations, make people's rewards dependent on achieving those results.
- **Anticipate potential obstacles** and develop contingency plans during the project's start-up phase.

Anticipate resources needed—When you're leading a project or team initiative, create an implementation plan. Identify the knowledge, skills, and competencies that people need to succeed and assess potential players against these criteria. Match the right players to the right roles and accountabilities. Identify the unique demands of the project, and then create coaching, training, and development plans to leverage people's strengths and address any gaps in competencies.

Track progress and outcomes—Establish criteria and measurement methods to track team results on a project or initiative. Establish both lead and lag measures because neither is sufficient by itself. Lead measures, or performance drivers, can provide early indications of success that allow you to adjust the plan, but they won't tell you whether you'll get the results you want. Lag measures won't deliver those early indications of success; they'll provide only the outcome of your implementation. In establishing measures, consider quantity, cost, customer satisfaction, number of errors, safety incidents, and timeliness. Choose measurable targets that will command people's attention and focus their energy on concrete action. Ask others for ideas on the best measures. Monitor results and make adjustments based on progress, barriers, and changes in the environment.

Make metrics:

- **Objective**—are focused on results important to the team and the organization.
- **Actionable**—give your team information they can act on.
- **Consistently trackable**—can be reliably monitored over time.
- **Easy to implement**—are readily available, not time- or labor-intensive to track.
- **Quantifiable**—can be represented as a number or percentage or date.
- **Relevant**—will reveal important trends, progress, and barriers.

Communicate your execution plan to mobilize the team—Besides being

12

operationally sound, your execution plan must inspire performance. Create a strategy for communicating your plan to contributors and stakeholders. Consider the objectives you want to achieve with each audience, your influence approach, and how you will deliver the communication. How can you encourage two-way communication to increase engagement? Set up processes to seek input and address ongoing concerns.

Seek feedback on your execution skills—Ask your peers, team members, or manager how you can better lead your team to execute priorities. Do people view you as someone who gets things done? If not, what obstacles do they observe? How can you create better plans and a stronger execution culture so people are more motivated and accountable for getting the right things done effectively? Ask what you do particularly well and then look for ways to apply your strengths and work on your development areas.

▶▶▶ Stretch It... Apply your execution skills in more challenging ways.

Align your priorities with those of other team leaders—Take responsibility for aligning priorities across teams. Work with other leaders to determine how each team will contribute to higher-level organization goals. Each leader should create objectives that are measurable, within the leader's influence, realistic, and time bound, and then present them to the other leaders and ask for feedback. Leaders also should consider whether, as a group, they cover the organization's priorities and check for overlap, conflicting goals, and opportunities for synergy.

Align individual performance goals with team priorities—Do the accountabilities in individual performance plans align with team priorities? If not, work with individuals on revised performance plans that reflect these goals. Clarify individual performance expectations that are driven by team priorities. Provide practical examples of how these priorities should guide decision making and actions. Also, make sure people know how individual performance ties to rewards and consequences. Recognize and reward them when they achieve expected results.

Identify a team priority you've been struggling to advance—If you're unable to realize a goal, diagnose the root cause and improve your execution plan. Seek coaching from an expert at driving projects to achieve results. Explain your plan and ask for feedback. Together, identify the strengths and weaknesses of your implementation by comparing your current plan to the Key Actions for this competency. Then, identify what you will do to improve your plan.

12

Support for developing Execution

Emotional Intelligence Essentials. It's critical for you to build trusting relationships with your team, internal partners, and stakeholders when you execute projects and lead strategic initiatives. People's personal needs for self-esteem, involvement, and respect are just as important as their practical needs, especially when you're pushing them to achieve challenging goals. Developing your interpersonal sensitivity will help you understand and empathize with others' emotions. How can you support and motivate anyone who might be struggling to achieve project results? You can strong-arm them into conforming to your execution plan, but for enduring, positive results, seek their involvement and commitment, not just their compliance.

Driving for Results. Successful execution requires more than great plans, clear accountability, and ongoing measurement. You'll need to set challenging goals from the outset to stretch your team's capabilities. Then, when team members face setbacks, encourage them to overcome barriers through problem solving, tenacity, and persistence.

12

13 Facilitating Change

Leading others through the implementation and
acceptance of improvements and change within
the workplace.

The Spirit of This Competency

This competency is about being a catalyst—someone who encourages others to
embrace changes and implement new ideas. As the world grows more complex,
being nimble and adapting at great speed are key competitive differentiators and
critical to responding to threats, challenges, and opportunities. To be successful,
you must champion your team's efforts to learn and innovate rapidly, creating a
team culture that anticipates change and supports constant reinvention.

Self-Insight Questions

How are you doing at Facilitating Change right now? Ask yourself:

- Do I clearly communicate when and why a change is coming?

- Am I sensitive to how my team might feel about making changes?

- How do I encourage others to commit to implementing better approaches?

- Do I invite others to share ideas and contribute to continuous improvement efforts?

- How do I reward and recognize people who make useful changes?

- How am I monitoring and measuring changes so I can tell if they're working?

Key Actions: Building Blocks for Success

Key Actions are behaviors that work together to help you demonstrate this competency effectively.

Communicate what is changing and why—Explain the need for change and what the benefits might be; emphasize how change will affect performance expectations and individual, team, and organizational results.

Address resistance—Ask questions to uncover others' opinions and feelings about change; respond with empathy.

Involve others—Seek and use others' ideas when implementing changes to build their commitment to a successful implementation.

Provide implementation support—Clarify direction, specify next steps, and offer resources; hold others responsible for implementing change; track progress and measure the impact of changes.

Reward change—Recognize and reward team members who take actions that support change; communicate your confidence in others' ability to make successful changes.

13

When you're facilitating change effectively, you'll notice:

Your team is committed to process improvement.

- Your team regularly challenges processes and assumptions to determine if they are necessary and efficient.
- You ask your team, "How can we do this better?" instead of imposing your solution.
- Recognition and reward systems promote continuous improvement and change.
- You and your team are willing to take risks in challenging the status quo.

Your team implements change initiatives smoothly.

- Team members are ready to implement a change because they understand its purpose and importance at the outset.
- People readily support changes because you are sensitive to their objections, anxieties, confusion, anger, and distrust.
- You communicate change initiatives early and clearly; the team understands "what's in it for me."
- Your team views change as an ongoing, integral part of everyone's job rather than as a crisis event.
- Team members are energized because change is implemented in a timely, efficient manner, and they see results improve.

There is a noticeable improvement in team performance.

- Your team measures results, and it's easy to see that efficiency, cost, and/or customer service indicators have improved.
- New and innovative products and services are creating customer demand.
- Team transformation—even small adjustments—becomes the norm.

13

Critical Leadership Moments

As a leader, you face situations, or **Critical Leadership Moments,** that stretch your skills. Facilitating Change can help you to:

Engage

▶ Help Others Accept Change

▶ Encourage Experimentation and New Ideas

Drive

▶ Make Change Happen

Facilitating Change is **essential** for success if you want to:

Help Others Accept Change

To manage the interpersonal challenges, resistance, and uncertainty that come with change initiatives, focus on these **Key Actions:**

- **Communicate what is changing and why** so the people affected by the change understand the reasons behind it and the expected benefits.

- **Address resistance** by asking questions to uncover others' opinions and feelings about the change and empathize with their concerns.

- **Involve others** in planning the implementation and solving problems by asking for their ideas.

Also see **Influencing** to be even better prepared for this Critical Leadership Moment.

Make Change Happen

To see progress and get results—despite the challenges and disruption that often come with change—focus on these **Key Actions:**

- **Involve others** by asking them to contribute ideas (rather than telling them what to do); they'll be more likely to commit to change.

- **Provide implementation support** to ensure progress. For example, make sure the team has clear plans, offer your support, and establish methods to track milestones.

- **Reward change** by recognizing and encouraging people with supportive attitudes and actions.

Also see **Execution** to be even better prepared for this Critical Leadership Moment.

13

Facilitating Change will **boost** your success if you want to:

Encourage Experimentation and New Ideas

While **Driving Innovation** is critical for encouraging fresh, new ideas, some of those ideas—especially bold ones—will encounter resistance and skepticism. Helping others through these challenging transitions is key to ensuring that your team is capable of the constant reinvention today's work environment demands.

13

⚠️ Common Mistakes

You can avoid common Facilitating Change errors by paying attention to how people react to your efforts.

Under Actions

When you don't demonstrate the Key Actions for Facilitating Change effectively, the results can be disappointing.

If you notice that:	You might be:	Try these quick remedies:
Your team defaults to "that's just how we do things around here"	Inadvertently accepting (or even advocating) old ways of thinking	• Recognize that you might be closed-minded or resistant and work at viewing change as an opportunity, not a threat. Just about every process has room for improvement, so constructively challenge legacy approaches. • If you tend to favor tradition or to be risk-averse, partner with a colleague who can nudge you out of your comfort zone.
Your team is confused about changes going on around them	Inadequately communicating the change	• Address the change early, but not abruptly. Be clear about what the change is, why it's happening, what outcomes are expected, and what team members' roles and accountabilities will be. Communicate throughout implementation to avoid uncertainty and head off rumors. • Ensure that your message describes the benefits to the organization, team, and individuals. Make sure the change is not perceived as a punishment.
Attempts to change fizzle out	Distracted or unfocused on key implementation steps	• You can sustain the team's energy and enthusiasm throughout the change process by measuring and communicating progress, (i.e., letting people know their efforts are paying off). Make the change a priority; show your commitment to achieving positive results.
People abandon change at the first sign of resistance	Missing the opportunity to create a safe environment for change	• Be candid about why the change is happening and encourage your team to get involved. Ask for and integrate their ideas. • Put yourself in the shoes of the people affected by change. Empathize with their fears and concerns. Recognize and reward their efforts to support the change.

13

Over Actions

When you demonstrate certain Facilitating Change Key Actions at an extreme level, it can lead to poor results.

If you notice that:	You might be:	Try these quick remedies:
Your team is in a constant state of flux	**Introducing too many changes**	• Focus on the changes that address high-priority problems. Involving too many people and opinions or changing for the sake of change might have a negative effect. • Monitor progress; set clear milestones and metrics, specifying the outcomes you expect and by when. Be willing to adjust quickly or abandon dead-end efforts.
People are reluctant to propose changes	**Expecting too much**	• Involve your team judiciously. Sometimes people don't have the background or perspective to offer viable suggestions, and they might feel pressure to suggest *something*. When people do make recommendations, don't be overly critical or punish ideas that fail.
Stakeholders question your commitment	**Over-sharing your concerns**	• Be an advocate for change. If you question a proposed change, seek information before sharing your concerns publicly—especially with senior leaders and stakeholders. • While empathizing with others and disclosing your thoughts about a change help to build your team's trust, appearing overly concerned can undermine the effort and affect your credibility as a leader.
Your team seems to be overwhelmed by the change	**Introducing the change too quickly or aggressively**	• Set realistic expectations for results and be patient. Changing people's attitudes and behavior takes time. Move slowly at first. Pick up the pace as people show acceptance and continually express confidence in their ability to sustain momentum. • Introduce a change with your team before it enters their world as a rumor. People can panic if they feel uninformed or overlooked. • Have a realistic implementation plan that includes the proper time, staff, funds, etc. Manage expectations (especially your own) on what is achievable. Seek your team's input on what they can accomplish and by when.

13

Development Activities

Some of these activities will help you quickly address Critical Leadership Moments. Others require a greater investment of time and resources and can be part of your longer-term development plan. Choose the activities that work best for your goals.

▶▷▷ Prepare for It... Prepare for opportunities to facilitate change.

Assess your reactions to change—Think about your reactions to past changes to understand how your attitude and behaviors might affect your team. Have you been a champion of change, indifferent, or a skeptic, and how can you manage your own resistance? Are your actions consistent with your messages about change? For example, do you reward people who question or suggest improvements to established work practices? What do you do—or not do—to help your team adjust, and what are the results? What is new or different about you, your team, or the organization that might affect how you react to change now versus the last time? Ask for input from peers, direct reports, managers, or others who have knowledge of your effort to manage change, and act on their feedback the next time you face change.

Anticipate your team's reactions to change—Plan for varied reactions. Some people might be cautious and reluctant, while others are comfortable with uncertainty; some might bring a pragmatic—even indifferent—perspective. Anticipate who might resist, why, and the degree of resistance before rolling out a new change to the team, especially if anyone is likely to be disruptive.

Brainstorm a list of pros and cons—Think through the effects of the change on you, the team, and stakeholders. What are the pros and cons of the change for each party? Consider what you can do to minimize the cons and make the pros more likely. Use your list of pros to address resistance and help others visualize a better future state.

Find a change mentor—Observe leaders or peers who seize opportunities for change, challenge the status quo, and manage the change process effectively. Seek coaching or mentoring from leaders like this. Ask for advice on a small change first, and then build the relationship with your mentor as you encounter more transformative, higher-stakes changes.

13

>>> **Try It...** Practice your skills in facilitating change.

Create a communication strategy—Formulate a clear, simple way to communicate the purpose and process of change, avoiding jargon or technical terminology. Identify everyone who will be affected and how the change will affect them. Choose a way to communicate with these people quickly and consistently with a message that can immediately help them feel comfortable with the change.

Address resistance—Don't guess or assume people's issues and concerns about a change. Interview or survey others—anonymously if necessary—to learn their candid views on an upcoming change. Ask what would make them feel more confident, at ease, or positive in relation to the change. Listen, empathize, and act on what you hear. Consider leveraging diverse opinions among your team members by asking them to ease one another's transition. For example, pair resistant team members with those more open to change or ask someone with little organizational change experience to partner with a person who's experienced quite a bit.

Establish a transition team—Your team is more likely to make a smooth transition if they are active in making the change happen. How can you leverage the enthusiasm of strong supporters or challenge the hesitant to take ownership of critical communications, tasks, and measurement steps? Ask for their ideas—and use them. Give people clear roles, empower them, and hold them accountable for specific outcomes—and to one another—throughout the transition.

Be proactive about change—Always be on the lookout for opportunities to improve and encourage your team to do the same. Create a standing agenda item in team meetings to analyze processes and brainstorm ways to simplify them. Establish a team culture of asking "why?" about work expected to be done a certain way or "why not?" about something that can't be done. Occasionally invite an unbiased observer (e.g., someone from a different department, a customer, etc.) to suggest where change is needed. What do they see that those too immersed in day-to-day operations cannot?

Create a rewards system—It's important to recognize and reward people who support and implement a change, especially because some changes require a longer-term, sustained commitment. Often, the rewards are spontaneous and sparse or sometimes overlooked as leaders focus on tactical steps. As you create a change implementation plan, think about what you can do to encourage people along the way, such as recognizing early adopters, people who offer ideas, or those who take on key responsibilities.

Be a change coach—People going through change often need careful guidance and advice, including how to behave in this new situation. Provide timely feedback and offer your support. Don't dump and run; be present and accessible. Observe people's feelings and reactions—not just when the change is introduced, but periodically as it's implemented. Step in to guide and encourage people when needed, without taking over or appearing to demand change. What techniques can you share with your team to ease burdens or address obstacles

13

.

>>> **Stretch It...** Apply your skills in facilitating change in more challenging ways.

Volunteer to support a major organizational transition—Get involved in the planning and process of an organization-wide change. Seek projects that require initiating, communicating, and planning the change, even if you play a small role. Find opportunities to work with a senior leader who has successfully led a change initiative. Ask him or her for guidance and feedback on techniques, tactics, and processes that you can use when leading a change initiative on your team.

Use failure as a learning opportunity—Conduct postmortems on unsuccessful changes or transitions. At what point did things head downhill? What could have been done differently? For example, was a change doomed by poor communications or lack of a clear implementation plan? What was the impact on individuals, the team, and the organization? Were those who supported the change and tried to get results rewarded for their efforts?

Volunteer to help a community organization make a change—Sometimes being an objective party might allow you more latitude to drive change than you'd have in your own organization. In a less-familiar environment, however, it's even more important to ask questions so you understand how people will react to the change and how the organization's current culture, practices, and strategic goals will support or complicate the change. What factors will ease the transition, and what might get in the way?

Invest in continuous learning—Stay abreast of the latest theories about change via books, articles, websites, podcasts, videos, and workshops. Many thought leaders and change experts develop change models. Look for a model you can apply to your situation (or compare a few to see which fits best). Be sure the model addresses:

- Rewarding people for their ideas.
- Addressing resistance to change.
- Communicating complex messages clearly.
- Evaluating all ideas before making a decision.
- Involving others in developing solutions.
- Gaining others' commitment to change.

13

Support for developing Facilitating Change

Emotional Intelligence Essentials. Change can make people feel uncertain or overwhelmed; they might question their capability. You can encourage them to try something new by creating a safe, trusting environment. Empathizing with others' concerns and expressing confidence in their abilities will boost their willingness to try new things. Inviting their ideas will help build their commitment, and offering your support shows that you're committed too.

Adaptability. Helping others through times of change often requires that you demonstrate your willingness to change and adapt. Being stringent or inflexible can cause difficulty for your team if they're asked to (or perhaps have chosen to) challenge old ways of thinking. Remind yourself to treat new situations as opportunities for improvement and growth. Encourage your team to do the same.

Continuous Learning. You or your team might resist change simply because you don't understand why it's necessary. By continually improving your skills and building your knowledge about your organization, industry, market, or internal processes and functions, you'll be better equipped to understand and advocate for changes. Likewise, having an appreciation for what the change is intended to achieve can reduce risk or fear of failure.

Driving for Results. Too often, change initiatives introduced with energy and enthusiasm can stall or fail because they place—if only for a short time—too many demands on time, funding, or staff. While it can be tempting to abandon the idea and revert to the "tried and true," it's important to stay focused on making the change. Be disciplined, make change a priority, and work to prevent resistance or distractions from interfering with your team's progress

13

14 Guiding Team Success

Building, motivating, and guiding a cohesive team.

The Spirit of This Competency

This competency is about building and maintaining high-performing teams—teams that can solve problems and navigate in new directions. Whether you're leading a team that's completing a short-term project or a long-term organizational initiative, your first step is to ensure that the team has a clearly defined role, responsibilities, and goals that will help it function efficiently and cohesively. Leaders who effectively guide their teams provide ongoing motivation, advocacy, and support. They demonstrate strong commitment to the team's purpose, yet also value each member's contribution.

Self-Insight Questions

How are you doing at Guiding Team Success right now? Ask yourself:

- How well do I communicate team objectives?
- How well do I clarify each team member's roles and responsibilities?
- Do I offer my time to help the team overcome barriers and resolve conflicts? Do I provide appropriate guidance and feedback?
- How do I inspire team cohesion?
- What have I done to celebrate and reward successful team performance?

Key Actions: Building Blocks for Success

Key Actions are behaviors that work together to help you demonstrate this competency effectively.

Develop direction—Clarify the purpose and importance of the team (e.g., through a team charter or mission statement). Set specific and measurable short- and long-term goals.

Develop structure—Clarify team members' roles and responsibilities. Put in place steering, review, and support functions.

Support the team—Build team members' sense of ownership and confidence by helping them generate ideas, make decisions, obtain resources, and overcome barriers. Advocate for team decisions with upper management. Celebrate team success.

Facilitate agreement—Ensure that discussions add value by confirming agreements and specifying next steps, needed resources and support, and how to track progress.

Involve others—Leverage others' skills and gain their support by asking for their ideas, opinions, and participation.

Inform the team—Share important information with the team. Review the team's results regularly and offer positive and developmental feedback.

14

When you're guiding team success effectively, you'll notice:

Team members are clear about their roles and the team's objectives.

- Each team member understands why the team was formed and what it's meant to accomplish.
- Team members understand their tasks and their expected level of performance.
- Team members are focused on a purpose higher than their individual performance; they share a common vision of where the team is going.

The team is performing to expectations or even higher.

- The team identifies skill gaps and works to fill them. Individuals' skills are complementary.
- Team members share information and ideas freely and proactively. They end the project with as much enthusiasm and willingness to contribute as they began it.
- The team has the support needed to overcome barriers and the confidence to pursue opportunities. You trust the team to make decisions without your direct input.
- Interactions among team members are positive; respect and comradery support collaboration.
- You let the members' strengths drive the team's direction.

You are closely involved with the team.

- When building the team, you determine and secure the resources and expertise they will need.
- You focus on developing team members as well as accomplishing the team's charter. You delegate tasks effectively and seek growth opportunities for team members.
- You stay in close communication with team members. Regardless of physical location, all team members feel connected and supported.

14

Critical Leadership Moments

As a leader, you face situations, or **Critical Leadership Moments,** that stretch your skills. Guiding Team Success can help you to:

Engage

▶ Challenge Your Team to Stretch Their Performance

▶ Establish Your Authority

▶ Be a Diversity Advocate

Drive

▶ Provide Team Structure and Direction

▶ Share More Responsibility with Your Team

▶ Focus the Team on Critical Business Priorities

Guiding Team Success is **essential** for success if you want to:

Challenge Your Team to Stretch Their Performance

To create a team environment that encourages your team members to strive for excellence, focus on these **Key Actions:**

- **Develop structure** so that team members' roles and responsibilities are clear, differentiated, and leverage each contributor's strengths. Make sure people know how and how often their work will be reviewed.

- **Support the team** by helping people feel ownership and self-confidence. Give them the authority to generate ideas, make decisions, and obtain resources. Offer your time to overcome barriers.

- **Inform the team** of results regularly and make sure they're meeting expectations. Offer positive feedback and encourage the team to strive for more. Offer developmental feedback to anyone getting off track.

Also see the **Coaching** competency to be even better prepared for this Critical Leadership Moment.

Provide Team Structure and Direction

To provide the team with the structure, role clarity, and guidance to accomplish key tasks, focus on these **Key Actions:**

- **Develop direction** that includes the purpose and importance of the team. Share a team charter or mission statement and establish specific and measurable short- and long-term goals.

- **Develop structure** so that the team members have clear roles and responsibilities. Identify who else is involved or who else in invested in the team's work (e.g., senior leadership, other stakeholders, mentors) and list resources available for help and direction.

- **Inform the team** of any details they'll need to know to be successful. Don't filter or censor information; candidly and regularly share information that will help the team make educated decisions. Let them know what they're doing well and where they can improve.

Also see the **Execution** competency to be even better prepared for this Critical Leadership Moment.

 Guiding Team Success will **boost** your success if you want to:

Establish Your Authority

While **Influencing** is essential for communicating your leadership agenda in a commanding and compelling manner, guiding your team toward important goals—without taking over—will show you have the confidence to let them shine. It's important to set clear goals, reinforce accountabilities, and monitor progress. The team's performance reflects on your leadership, so provide feedback and redirect efforts if the team is heading off course.

Be a Diversity Advocate

While **Creating an Inclusive Environment** is essential for building a team culture that acknowledges, respects, and celebrates people's differences, you should keep diversity in mind as you build, deploy, and direct teams. Choose team members with complementary skills, and invite everyone to share ideas and opinions, even those that defy tradition or consensus. Advocate for new and different ideas.

Share More Responsibility with Your Team

While **Delegation and Empowerment** is essential for confidently delegating key responsibilities to your team members, guiding your team toward a group objective often requires sharing responsibilities with several team members. Define each person's responsibilities and ensure that tasks do not clash. Offer opportunities, support, and guidance to every team member, not an exclusive few.

Focus the Team on Critical Business Priorities

While **Execution** is essential for reaching critical organizational goals, teams—rather than select individuals—often are deployed to achieve those goals. The team is destined to fail if it lacks a clear purpose at the outset. Rally the team around its short- and long-term goals, and show how its work connects to broader organizational priorities. Establish how and when to measure the team's progress.

14

⚠ Common Mistakes

You can avoid common errors when Guiding Team Success by paying attention to how people react to your efforts.

Under Actions

When you don't demonstrate the Key Actions for Guiding Team Success effectively, the results can be disappointing.

If you notice that:	You might be:	Try these quick remedies:
The team seems frenetic and uncoordinated	Failing to communicate a team mission	• Do team members understand what they're being asked to do and why? Explain the linkages between their contributions and organizational success. • Find out where team members are spending their time and redirect, if needed. Are they pursuing their own interests? Are they prioritizing the right things?
There's confusion over who's doing what	Poorly defining roles and responsibilities	• Define each person's role on the team. Explain how you'll measure performance and get everyone's agreement to accountabilities. • Differentiate roles to ensure that all tasks are accomplished.
Some people do everything; some do hardly anything	Playing favorites	• Don't rely on one or two people to carry out the work. Examine your biases to see how you involve people. • Avoid giving preferential treatment to high performers. This can dissolve team unity and morale.
Team members seem clueless or ill-informed	Withholding valuable information	• Disclose information to build the team's trust. Share early and often. • Communicate information broadly and consistently. Be sure to include people with less experience and those who work remotely.
The team takes the same approach every time	Favoring the status quo	• Give your team room to experiment as long as their ideas align with organizational objectives. • Keep up with changing organizational priorities by creating a fresh project plan and team charter for every new opportunity.

14

If you notice that:	You might be:	Try these quick remedies:
Your team is missing deadlines	**Ineffectively monitoring or measuring results**	• Set clear expectations for how and when to measure results. • Make progress reports—team and individual—routine communications. Explain results and be open to periodically revising metrics, accountabilities, and timelines.
The team gets stuck	**Neglecting to provide support**	• Pay attention to the team. Lack of regular contact can hinder your ability to monitor team performance and help to overcome barriers.

Over Actions

When you demonstrate certain Guiding Team Success Key Actions at an extreme level, it can lead to poor results.

If you notice that:	You might be:	Try these quick remedies:
Team members aren't engaged	**Taking over**	• Trust your team to make decisions without your direct input as long as they have the right resources and information. • Invite your team to problem solve. You might spend more time than doing it yourself, but you'll build commitment and ownership.
Team members are in over their heads	**Expecting too much**	• Help the team set achievable goals. Check in often to make sure tasks are manageable. • Consider the risks before you take your team into an area where you or they might lack expertise. • Is a project getting bigger and more demanding? Monitor outside forces and stakeholder requests, and then manage expectations.
You are frequently measuring progress and outcomes	**Fixated on results**	• Set realistic measures: What will you measure, and how often? Who sees the results? Some trends take time to evolve, so checking data too often can lead to panic and premature actions. • Manage stakeholders' expectations. What information is essential to share, and when? Too-frequent updates can be overwhelming. • Choose measurement metrics that evaluate both task- and people-related outcomes.

14

Development Activities

Some of these activities will help you quickly address Critical Leadership Moments. Others require a greater investment of time and resources and can be part of your longer-term development plan. Choose the activities that work best for your goals.

▶▷▷ Prepare for It... Prepare for opportunities to guide team success.

Stay connected to organizational priorities—Even if a priority has no obvious connection to your team, network with senior leaders and stay close to strategic decisions. Share what you know with your team. Include examples of how they are supporting the organization's mission and demonstrating its values. Heightened awareness will make the team more likely to support these priorities.

Build team members' skills—What skills will your team need to support upcoming initiatives? Innovation? Collaboration? You might conduct a skills inventory to identify gaps, and then set development goals and identify activities to enhance team members' competence and confidence. Plan cross-training, mentoring, and stretch assignments to expand team members' skill sets. Discover how these individuals like to learn and then find ways to accommodate their similarities and differences.

Review job descriptions—Can your team cover all the roles it needs to be successful? Are some people going unrecognized for their responsibilities? In advance of a project or task, develop baseline expectations for various roles so you can make the best assignments when the time comes. Involve your team in setting expectations for each position on the team. If role or job descriptions already exist, review them for accuracy.

Understand the team ecosystem—Investigate how teams in your organization work together. Your team's success often depends on contributions or support from other teams. Learn more about others' agendas and team charters. Are there synergies or conflicts with your team? You might join cross-functional teams, attend other groups' meetings, or network with the teams' leaders. Identify your shared goals. Consider resource sharing (people, equipment) and look for ways your teams can increase or improve their interactions.

Determine obstacles to success—In past projects or team initiatives, which organizational systems (hiring, training, compensation/rewards, communication, etc.), processes, or policies supported or hindered your team's progress? Does your team have unique circumstances? Are there situations in which you might bend the rules for your team or use different approaches or metrics? Discuss with your manager.

14

▶▶▶ **Try It...** Practice guiding team success.

Engage the team—Be open to team members' ideas, approaches, and suggestions, and ask for others' opinions before sharing yours. Evaluate proposed solutions together: Assign each team member a partner; one person researches and presents the pros of a solution, and the other shares the cons. Together, they offer a recommendation, which the rest of the team can build on.

Have a project plan—Treat each team initiative as a project with a beginning, middle, and end. Give each phase well-defined and measurable objectives and clear tasks, roles, start/end times, and resources. Every person on the project should understand the full scope of the plan, not just his or her piece. Adjust project-planning tools to account for often-overlooked steps, such as giving feedback and celebrating successes. At critical points, reevaluate the plan and adjust as needed.

Connect team and organizational priorities—Incorporate organizational, group, and team goals into team members' work expectations or performance plans. Cascade objectives from senior or strategic leaders, and create SMART goals—specific, measurable, attainable, relevant, and time bound. Check progress regularly and provide balanced feedback. Do your team members feel connected to the organization's priorities? If not, find out what's getting in the way and provide support to overcome obstacles.

Pay attention to what's going on—Even if you lead a well-performing team, monitor their performance metrics. Explore qualitative information as actively and frequently as the quantitative; balance team member's perspectives with the numbers. Ask what's really going on and explore underlying causes if the team is heading off course. Listen for conflict, problems, or misgivings. Stay close tactfully, avoiding micromanagement.

Promote the team—Promote the team's latest project or initiative. Use visuals, symbols, and slogans to generate awareness and energy around the team's goals. Consider using a catchy title that creates affiliation, promise, and energy. Arrange off-site team meetings or fun activities to promote team spirit. Leverage organizationwide communications to promote the project and to share the team's accomplishments.

Schedule routine check-ins with the team—View team meetings and updates as priorities, despite other demands on your time. Don't depend on team communications software—let your team hear and see you and ask you questions in person. Always include an agenda item to identify barriers to team success and end with clear next steps related to securing support and resources.

14

Evaluate the flow of information—Does your team feel in the know or in the dark? Ask them how you can improve communications. What about the type of information you share? Is it relevant? Too much? Not enough? Provide the information needed to build trust and improve morale while also supporting organizational decisions and objectives. Then, make it easy for your team to access important updates.

Keep stakeholders informed—Involve key stakeholders in establishing metrics and measurement approaches. Ask what they need to know and when and how they prefer to receive information. Manage stakeholders' expectations so you're not overcommitting your team. Be clear about when the team can make adjustments and when it's simply too late. Occasionally, invite stakeholders to your team meetings and allocate time for them to share observations and suggestions.

Celebrate success—Recognize and reward accomplishments to keep your team inspired, motivated, and committed to excellence. Focus on team success over any one person's contributions. Regularly publish accomplishments and share the information prominently. Use a variety of recognition methods. For example, team members might write acknowledgments for one another. Celebrate milestones, not just final outcomes. Surprise your team with informal celebrations or formal recognition.

>>> **Stretch It...** Guide team success in more challenging ways.

Reflect on your team leadership skills—Evaluate how successfully you led your team on a recent project. Do a candid self-evaluation, then ask team members for feedback on your leadership skills—including each Key Action for this competency—using a multirater survey. Use the results to target your development. As you develop and lead new teams or projects, ask for frequent, informal feedback. What metrics will show if your skills are improving and having an impact on your team's success? Does morale, efficiency, or customer satisfaction steadily improve?

Consider alternative team structures—Partnerships, star points, alliances, and self-directed teams are less common ways to bring people together in support of a common objective. Teammates' roles can be less familiar, but they also allow for greater latitude. Get involved in—or encourage your team to try—different ways of working together and across boundaries. Uncommon team structures can be empowering and motivating, as often they demand increased accountability.

Create the desired state—What's your vision for how your team will operate one year from now? Create an action plan to get there. Identify the resources (human, financial, or physical) you'll need. Who else needs to be involved in making your vision a reality, and how will you gain their support? Identify existing systems (selection, training, compensation/rewards, communication, performance management, etc.) that support or hinder your vision. Work with your manager to remove barriers.

14

Observe how other leaders develop successful teams—Identify people you admire for their team leadership skills. Look for ways to work with them and identify skills you can learn from them. Discuss approaches that have worked well for keeping teams productive and engaged. If you can't work directly with a particular leader, approach established teams that consistently meet their goals and have excellent morale and low turnover.

Guide a new or different team—If you're getting too comfortable using the same plans and processes for every team project, look for an opportunity to lead a new or different team. At work, consider cross-functional, interdisciplinary, or interdepartmental teams; outside work, community, charitable, cultural, business, or political organizations might need leadership. In either situation, establish team goals, roles, responsibilities, and methods to track and measure progress. Consider coaching a sports team.

Come to the rescue of a struggling team—Volunteer to assist a team improve direction, cohesiveness, or performance. What might you do to reinvigorate their efforts? What advice can you give? Consider co-leading with a peer who has an overwhelming workload or is struggling to motivate his or her team.

Support for developing Guiding Team Success

Emotional Intelligence Essentials. Successful teams are founded on trust. Your intentions and actions cannot come across as self-serving. Be ready to offer your support and quickly address anything that's getting in your team's way. Build team members' sense of ownership by involving them. Ask for—and use—their ideas.

Adaptability. Guiding your team toward achieving their goals is rarely a linear path. Plans, resources, and expectations change. To help your team persist despite setbacks or confusion, find out the rationale behind changes in direction and explain it to your team. Look for and communicate the benefits of changing course, then make the changes quickly.

Driving for Results. With competing priorities, teams can lose direction and enthusiasm, and projects can become stagnant. As the team's leader and visionary, be tenacious about reaching goals. Don't let irrelevant issues get in the way. Help the team maintain momentum by measuring and sharing their results.

14

15 Influencing

Using persuasion strategies to gain acceptance
of ideas and commitment to actions.

The Spirit of This Competency

Have you ever needed to get something done, but failed because other people
didn't agree with you or feel the same sense of urgency? Your success as a leader
depends on your ability to gain commitment from others—direct reports, peers,
managers, and external partners—to get work done. Do you need to rally support
from stakeholders or senior leaders? Do you want to persuade people to try a
new idea or accept a change? Or maybe you need to convince team members to
volunteer for an urgent project. With strong influencing skills, you'll handle these
challenging situations with confidence.

Self-Insight Questions

How are you doing at Influencing right now? Ask yourself:

- Do I miss opportunities to lobby for ideas that I believe in?
- Do I take the time to understand other people's goals before I try to influence them?
- Do I leave negotiations feeling like I conceded too much?
- Do I balance advocating for my position with asking questions to understand others?
- Do I struggle to figure out why I can influence some audiences but not others?

Key Actions: Building Blocks for Success

Key Actions are behaviors that work together to help you demonstrate this competency effectively.

Clarify the situation—Ask questions to explore issues, identify decision makers, and understand others' goals and concerns.

Share your perspective to build trust—Disclose your goals, experiences, and insights to encourage open discussion.

Build a compelling case—Tailor your persuasion strategy to engage people emotionally and rationally; use supporting evidence to communicate benefits and address any objections you anticipate.

Involve others in exploring solutions—Ask for others' ideas and then build on them to reach a solution people agree on.

Empathize with others' concerns—Listen when others share their feelings. Identify the facts and emotions they express to overcome their resistance and help them feel understood.

Steer commitment to action—Gauge whether others are ready to commit to action. Check that everyone understands next steps and responsibilities. Offer support.

15

When you're influencing effectively, you'll notice:

Others are sold on the value of your idea or plan.

- People clearly see how your idea or plan of action links to the work group's goals and values. They can state the benefits in terms of individual, team, and organizational performance improvements. They persuade others who are neutral or skeptical to commit to the initiative.

- As you present your business case, you notice people in your audience leaning forward, nodding, making continuous eye contact with you, and staying alert and interested.

- People convince themselves through active involvement with your idea. They experience its impact, importance, and practicality.

People aren't just complying, they're committed.

- After you discuss an idea or plan of action with your audience, they walk away feeling like they're part of the solution or even thinking that they, instead of you, initiated the idea.

- You ask open-ended questions to reveal new ideas, perspectives, and rationale. You ask provocative questions to get to the core of a problem. You help others discover the implications, so they reach their own conclusions.

- You aren't afraid of dissenters. Instead, you seek and respect conflicting viewpoints and build rapport by stressing the goals you share. When people raise objections or concerns, you're able to soften their resistance. You listen and respond with empathy, addressing both the facts and emotions they've expressed.

- You tap into your audience's emotions. You understand how they're feeling and adapt your approach to evoke reactions that build their commitment to your idea.

You can rely on others to see your plan through to success.

- You end your persuasive discussion with a call to action. People agree to take significant steps toward the final goal, including agreeing on specific responsibilities, time frames, and tracking methods. You gain initial concessions, which later turn into full commitments.

- After you present your business case, others begin talking in the future tense, referring to how things will be when the idea or change happens. They ask questions about next steps and their roles in the process. They take ownership of the actions and outcomes.

15

Critical Leadership Moments

As a leader, you face situations, or **Critical Leadership Moments,** that stretch your skills. Influencing can help you to:

Partner

▶ Gain Stakeholders' Support

▶ Navigate Organizational Politics

▶ Build Relationships Outside Your Organization

Engage

▶ Establish Your Authority

▶ Coach an Employee with a Performance Problem

▶ Help Others Accept Change

 Influencing is **essential** for success if you want to:

Gain Stakeholders' Support

To gain support from stakeholders when you don't have position power, focus on these **Key Actions:**

- **Clarify the situation** to understand stakeholders' perspectives, goals, and concerns.
- **Build a compelling case** that addresses stakeholders' unique needs and expectations.
- **Involve others in exploring solutions** to improve the odds of gaining their commitment.

Also see the **Building Partnerships** competency to be even better prepared for this Critical Leadership Moment.

Establish Your Authority

To communicate your leadership agenda in a commanding and compelling manner, focus on these **Key Actions:**

- **Steer commitment to action** to ensure that others are clearly accountable for next steps.
- **Share your perspective to build trust,** as candidly disclosing your position and motivations can boost others' confidence in your leadership.
- **Build a compelling case** by thoroughly researching facts and potential solutions, and confidently addressing any resistance.

Also see the **Guiding Team Success** competency to be even better prepared for this Critical Leadership Moment.

15

Influencing will **boost** your success if you want to:

Navigate Organizational Politics

While **Building Partnerships** is critical for appealing to various leaders across the organization, Influencing is often needed to gain support and commitment from those leaders.

Build Relationships Outside Your Organization

While **Building Partnerships** is critical for establishing and sustaining collaborative relationships with external partners, your influencing skills often are needed to persuade those outside your organization to see the value of the partnership.

Coach a Person with a Performance Problem

While **Coaching** is critical for guiding a person to improve, your influencing skills can convince the person that a change in performance is needed or that making a change will be beneficial.

Help Others Accept Change

While **Facilitating Change** is critical for managing the interpersonal challenges that often accompany change, Influencing is key to helping others see the benefits of accepting or implementing an organizational change.

15

⚠️ Common Mistakes

You can avoid common Influencing errors by paying attention to how people react to your efforts.

Under Actions

When you don't demonstrate the Key Actions for Influencing effectively, the results can be disappointing.

If you notice that:	You might be:	Try these quick remedies:
Your ideas fizzle out at the first sign of resistance	**Giving in too easily**	• Anticipate objections before presenting your idea or plan and be prepared to clearly describe your desired outcomes. • Listen carefully to others and use appropriate influence strategies to address resistance. Keep in mind that people naturally resist new ideas (even great ones) that represent change. • Try another approach if one influencing strategy isn't working.
You leave discussions feeling that you've gained agreement, but then nothing gets done	**Leaving things unresolved**	• Make sure you're closing the discussion effectively. Simply presenting a new plan or idea doesn't guarantee action. • Before ending the discussion, provide a clear summary, do a final check for agreement, and make sure that everyone knows the next steps.
You influence people well in certain situations, but struggle in others	**Relying on one influence strategy**	• Think about what matters to your audience and adapt your influencing strategy to engage both their emotional and rational needs. For example, your boss might need you to show research demonstrating the feasibility of your project, while your team might need to understand how the project will benefit them.
You struggle to get people to commit to your project or idea	**Dismissing others' thoughts and ideas**	• Keep an open mind, show respect and appreciation for others' ideas and contributions, and encourage people's involvement. • Use others' ideas whenever possible. While it can be a struggle to accept other people's thoughts and ideas when you have your own vision, you need them to have a personal stake in success. Besides, they might have creative ideas you hadn't thought of.

15

Over Actions

When you demonstrate certain Influencing Key Actions at an extreme level, it can lead to poor results.

If you notice that:	You might be:	Try these quick remedies:
People seem skeptical about your ideas and are asking many questions about feasibility	**Overselling your ideas**	• Present facts, expert opinions, and potential downsides. Help others understand the value of your idea by clearly describing the outcomes you expect and then encouraging discussion. • Minimize exaggerations that might make your ideas seem implausible, increase people's skepticism, and undermine their trust in you. When people commit to an idea, they want to feel that they made the choice based on their judgment, not your hard sell.
People are avoiding you, expressing anger, or lying about progress on projects	**Confusing coercion with influence**	• Use appropriate interpersonal techniques to gain agreement rather than forcing it. By pressuring people to adopt your idea or plan, you miss opportunities to inspire both their commitment and their ideas about ways to make the plan work. • Consider how you pose consequences. If you push through your ideas by threatening, disciplining, or withholding rewards from people who disagree with you, then you're coercing—not influencing—them. Such tactics could permanently damage your work relationships.
People don't take you seriously	**Using flattery to win favor**	• Offer only sincere praise to build strong, honest relationships. • Avoid giving exaggerated or insincere compliments. This approach shows a lack of respect for others, and they'll soon see through such tactics.
You feel that you must omit certain information or change it to gain buy-in from others	**Manipulating information**	• Keep your case strong by backing it with unbiased data. As a project moves forward, facts are inevitably revealed, and others will see you as untrustworthy if they discover you manipulated information. • Be completely honest, even when you're disclosing negative information. You'll inspire trust and confidence, and people will be more likely to adopt your ideas and plans.

15

Development Activities

Some of these activities will help you quickly address Critical Leadership Moments. Others require a greater investment of time and resources and can be part of your longer-term development plan. Choose the activities that work best for your goals.

▶▷▷ Prepare for It... Prepare for opportunities to influence others.

Clarify the benefits—Before you present an idea, recommendation, or plan, identify what you want to achieve and how you'll demonstrate the benefits. Be prepared to explain what each person will gain. Do you need people to commit to sharing their time or expertise? Then clarify how their contributions will help achieve goals that will benefit them. Do you need senior leaders to invest resources? Then demonstrate the expected return on their investment. Do you need to convince a person to improve performance? Then explain how improvements will help the individual's and the team's results.

Know your audience—Research people's backgrounds and ask questions so you understand your key stakeholders' perspectives. Do you understand their most pressing needs and the issues they're currently facing? Do you know their past positive and negative experiences with similar ideas or plans? Anticipate people's feelings and expect objections and reservations. Most people will tell you about their problems and priorities if you ask them careful, probing questions and then listen closely. The more you empathize with their situation, the more information you'll uncover. Adjust your persuasion strategy and communications to address their priorities.

Do your homework—Conduct background research and use your findings as you prepare persuasive presentations. Focus on statistics, reports, relevant articles, blogs, and expert opinions to support your business case. Look for evidence that demonstrates the outcomes—both positive and negative—most important to your stakeholders. Make sure your expertise matches that of your audience, so you're ready to address any detailed questions or objections.

Watch persuasive communicators and negotiators in action—Who are some leaders with strong influence skills, either within or outside your organization? Notice how they use facts and emotions to influence opinions. Ask what works well for them and what they might do differently and why. Note the specific behaviors that you might try. Also, note the behaviors you'd avoid.

15

Ask a persuasive leader to coach you—When you're preparing for an important meeting or presentation, ask your coach to evaluate your influencing strategy and give you feedback on its strengths and weaknesses. Have you identified the important decision makers? Does your persuasion approach address the unique needs of each one? What objections or resistance should you anticipate that you haven't prepared for? Ask for specific suggestions for improvement.

▶▶▷ **Try It...** Practice your influencing skills.

Base your influencing strategy on your strengths—If you're strong in analysis, use facts and logic to persuade others; if collaboration is your element, use your relationships to gain commitment. Innovative and creative? Use your ideas to generate excitement.

Make your message engaging—Create visuals, symbols, and slogans to reinforce the goals you share with your audience. Try some analogies to emphasize major points and to make the message more interesting. Can you tell a story to demonstrate your point? Are there questions you can ask the audience to solicit examples that can illustrate your ideas?

Test your ideas—Find people who don't have a big stake in the outcome of your solution. Explain your influencing strategy and gather their feedback on your ideas. Ask them to assume the roles of your stakeholders and raise possible objections and concerns. Practice listening, empathizing, and responding to their resistance. If they have connections to any of your stakeholders, ask for their help in getting support for your efforts.

Rehearse your persuasive presentation—Record yourself as you run through your presentation. Practice disclosing your goals to build trust. Then, present your recommendations and business case. Rehearse the questions you'll ask to involve your audience and to help them reach their own conclusions. Then, critique your influencing skills, noting what you do or say that's effective or ineffective compared to the key actions of this competency.

Display self-confidence and personal conviction—In upcoming meetings and discussions, strive to state your recommendations and rationale with more self-assurance. Instead of saying "I think," say "I know." Avoid minimizing your ideas or contributions by being too modest. Use more nonverbals—posture, facial expressions, mannerisms—that project confidence. Maintain eye contact. Practice using gestures to dramatize your points.

15

Ask open-ended questions to involve people—When persuading others, questions are your most powerful tool. Plan your questions before your presentation or discussion. How will you explore your stakeholders' perspectives, needs, and goals? How will you urge them to share their ideas and recommendations for resolving issues? What can you ask to encourage them to divulge their concerns and fears? Show your respect and appreciation for their responses and contributions, regardless of their roles, so that people feel valued and understood. Listen attentively to the questions people ask.

Address conflicts, problems, and misgivings directly but tactfully—Listen for the emotions behind people's comments or arguments. Through words and actions, show you understand how they feel; don't dismiss or ignore their objections or negative feelings. Distinguish your and others' wants from needs. Give up your wants to meet others' needs.

Practice speaking in informal settings—Ask an experienced, effective presenter to observe one of your persuasive presentations and give you feedback. What are your strengths and your areas for improvement? How can you improve the way you present your influencing strategy and business case? How can you increase audience involvement? How could you better anticipate and then respond to audience objections? After you've incorporated the person's suggestions, practice speaking again and reassess your performance.

▶▶▶ **Stretch It...** Apply your influencing skills in more challenging ways.

Lead an important stakeholder meeting or presentation—Designate a particularly persuasive audience member as an observer and coach. Ask this person to give you feedback after your presentation. Request specific, behavioral suggestions for improvement.

Join cross-functional, interdisciplinary, interdepartmental, or customer task forces or teams—Look for every opportunity to influence new stakeholders and partners. Find occasions to lead persuasive discussions with diverse groups or individuals.

Seek projects that require increasingly greater levels of influence—Try out different influencing techniques that push the boundaries of your comfort zone. Ask people to give you feedback so you know which skills are working and which you need to sharpen.

15

Volunteer for a project in which you have little or no authority—Build relationships as you establish your expertise and credibility with a goal of gaining people's commitment to getting the work done.

Build new strategic alliances with internal or external partners—Challenge yourself to work with a new and different audience so that you must learn more about people's perspectives and expectations before you try to influence them.

Lead a community, charitable, or political organization—These roles require influencing others to accomplish project goals and are a great opportunity to practice your skill in a setting outside work.

Support for developing Influencing

Emotional Intelligence Essentials. Getting buy-in and commitment from others is easier when you address their personal needs. Your practical, logical arguments can be convincing, but making strong interpersonal connections is important too.

Adaptability. People sometimes hesitate to agree because they feel uncertain or are simply unwilling to make a change or try something new. It's up to you to understand—and adapt to—their motivations, experiences, work styles, and perspectives. When you show you can adapt (and encourage others to do so), you model how being open to new and different experiences can lead to more opportunity.

Driving for Results. Influencing efforts can take time. Situations can be complicated, and many involve multiple stakeholders. Being persistent, despite delays, setbacks, or resistance, can be an advantage.

15

16 Personal Effectiveness Competencies

Adaptability, Continuous Learning,
and Driving for Results

How Can Personal Effectiveness Competencies Help or Hinder Your Success?

Success as a leader takes more than just demonstrating the impeccable interpersonal, management, and leadership skills covered in Chapters 4–15. Most great leaders also have a "certain something"—a special style or unique behavior patterns that set them apart. They might be especially flexible, curious, or tenacious. Other leaders can be skilled but still struggle; they have certain tendencies that lead to ineffective behaviors.

Personal Effectiveness competencies account for those tendencies. They deal with the individual preferences that can drive a leader's effectiveness—or, sometimes, derail it. This chapter covers three of the most important Personal Effectiveness competencies for leadership success: Adaptability, Continuous Learning, and Driving for Results.

Addressing Your Tendencies: A Different Approach to Development

Overcoming tendencies, especially those ingrained over time, means trying new approaches or developing new habits. It can be difficult, but it's not impossible.

Like other competencies, those related to your personal effectiveness are based on Key Actions. They are skills that can be practiced and improved, even if your tendencies conflict with them. Remember, however, that your tendencies can be difficult to change because they:

- Are based on early life experiences.
- Are comforting and familiar.
- Often become a problem only during stressful situations, periods of change, or when you take on higher levels of responsibility.

Overcome Negative Tendencies: Focus on Positive Behavior

Often, it's best to attack the negative behaviors associated with a tendency rather than the tendency itself. For example, if you are generally uncomfortable with change, you might show resistance when a change arises at work. Your example might even encourage your team to be skeptical too.

You can alter your behavior by learning more about the proposed change and its benefits. At first, keeping silent about your concern will be difficult to do, but a conscious behavior change—taking the time to learn more—will eventually cause others to perceive you differently.

As you read this chapter, think about your own tendencies: Which are helping—or hindering—your effectiveness? If you discover that your behavior patterns might be getting in your way, you can address them directly:

- Invite feedback on your strengths as well as your risk areas through behavioral assessment, personality inventories, and multirater feedback. The more self-awareness you gain, the more you'll avoid surprises and blind spots.
- Solicit help to overcome negative tendencies from coaches, trusted confidants (people who are safe but frank), and those in your daily work life whom your behavior affects.
- Surround yourself with people who are strong in your weaker tendencies.
- Stay aware of situations that trigger your worst tendencies and think about how to adjust your behavior.

Adaptability

Adjusting effectively to change by exploring the benefits, trying new approaches, and collaborating with others to make the change successful.

The Spirit of This Competency

This competency is about making transitions quickly and effectively when you face changing work demands, such as shifting responsibilities, staff, technology, or business strategies. There's nothing routine about leadership, and to be adaptable you need to effectively anticipate and handle complex and ambiguous situations. This means adjusting quickly and positively when you get new information or face opportunities and challenges. Also important is your willingness to suspend judgment and avoid being resistant. Instead, you'll need to rally others to adopt new ideas and to smoothly change course when appropriate.

 Key Actions: Building Blocks for Success

Key Actions are behaviors that work together to help you demonstrate this competency effectively.

Try to understand changes—Actively seek information (from coworkers, leaders, customers, competitors, technologies, and regulations) to understand the rationale and implications for changes.

Approach change with a positive mind-set—Treat new situations as opportunities for learning or growth; look for and communicate the benefits of changes; collaborate with others to implement changes.

Adjust your behavior—Quickly modify your approaches to deal effectively with changes; don't persist with ineffective methods; leverage available resources to ease the transition.

16

Adaptability Can Boost Other Skills

Like other Personal Effectiveness competencies, Adaptability skills can be extremely beneficial. They help you to nimbly and calmly adjust to complex situations, changing expectations, and new opportunities. Adaptability can support your development and enhance your performance in competencies such as:

- Creating an Inclusive Environment
- Decision Making
- Delegation and Empowerment
- Driving Innovation
- Facilitating Change
- Guiding Team Success
- Influencing

How adaptable are you?

If you readily adjust to change, you:

- Aren't surprised when change occurs and, in fact, you welcome it.
- Question why processes and business plans are stagnant; lack of change makes you uncomfortable.
- Are politically astute and can form new partnerships to ensure a smooth transition during times of change.
- Frame challenges in a positive way using constructive language.
- Maintain or improve your and your team's productivity during and after the change. You focus on results and stay the course to see change through.

Could you be more adaptable?

If you struggle to adjust when something is new or different, your tendencies and behaviors could be getting in the way of your success.

Just about every leader has struggled when faced with change. Change can happen so quickly that even a slight tendency to be uncomfortable or resist can affect your success. Which of your tendencies help you? Which get in the way of your desired results, and what can you do to improve?

Effective Behaviors	Troublesome Tendencies	Temper Your Tendencies
Do you:	Instead, do you:	Try this:
Actively seek information?	• Make assumptions? • Try to appear "in the know" even if you aren't? • View asking questions as challenging authority or as an admission that you lack knowledge? • Lack the patience to gather information? • Accept a change you don't agree with to avoid being disruptive?	• Clarify what's behind the change. Is it meant to solve a problem or take advantage of an opportunity? Find out the who, what, where, when, why, and how to fully understand the change. You might adjust your reaction once you know more. • Stay true. Being adaptable doesn't mean abandoning your priorities. Don't let assumptions cloud your perspective. Clarify any aspects of the change that seem to conflict with your leadership agenda, personal values, or team objectives.
Understand and communicate the benefits of change?	• Dismiss a change before trying to see its benefits? • Display a pessimistic or skeptical attitude? • Believe that past changes weren't worth the hassle? • Panic or assume the worst? • Let your team's resistance influence you? • Lack the confidence to advocate for the change?	• Someone thinks the change is a good idea, so find out the origins of the change and learn more about stakeholders' intentions. Share what you learn with your team. • Evaluate the pros and cons of the change. There are bound to be benefits you're not seeing or your biases are obscuring. Involve your team in looking critically at the situation the change is meant to improve. • Review your communications about the change. Position information positively and show your advocacy. Include at least two or three benefits of the change (using facts, not opinions) that your team can relate to.
Treat new situations as opportunities for learning or growth?	• Find changes to be more trouble than they're worth? • Take comfort in the status quo? • Prefer predictability and routine? • Feel bothered when asked to take on a challenge?	• Identify how the change might allow you or someone on your team to build skills. If the change is new to everyone, is there one person who can become the team's expert or coach? Challenge the team: "How can this change make us better?" • People often resist because they feel unprepared or set up to fail. Find out and quickly provide the support your team needs. • Consider your career track. If you want to be promoted or take on more responsibilities, be open to new assignments.

16

Effective Behaviors	Troublesome Tendencies	Temper Your Tendencies
Do you:	Instead, do you:	Try this:
Collaborate with others to implement changes?	• Think, "I'm in charge. We'll do this my way"? • Find it easier to do things yourself than to involve others? • Get involved in every aspect of implementation? • Hesitate to ask for help?	• Don't dictate actions. Your organization might say what needs to change and when, but your team likely can choose how. Encourage people to be creative. • Ask for help from people with expertise. Your partners in HR, Finance, and other areas can offer advice and resources.
Quickly modify your behavior?	• Prefer to wait and see? • Procrastinate or become defensive? • Choose the most conservative option? • Make only symbolic gestures? • Cling to the tried and true? • Have a tough time handling unexpected outcomes?	• Put your energy into making the change succeed instead of pointing out why it won't work. • Clearly communicate the change to your team right away; don't let rumors start. • Don't encourage or allow your team to stick with old ways. Hold people accountable for doing their part and make sure you have accountabilities too. • Be open to experimentation. Accept—even expect—some degree of failure, but don't let disappointment linger. Revise the plan and move on.

Development Activities

Developing Personal Effectiveness competencies is a balance of counteracting detrimental tendencies with constructive behavior. The following development activities for Adaptability can guide improvements in your self-awareness, skills, and behavior. They also can be part of your longer-term development plan.

▷▷▷ Assess your strengths and development needs:

• Ask for feedback on what others have observed you doing during times of change. Insist on balanced feedback that includes your strengths and opportunities for improvement. Find out your blind spots, be conscious of them, and develop alternative strategies.

- In what situations have you found it difficult to adapt to change? Reflect on your emotional reactions and try to identify the origin of your fears, anger, or even excitement about a change. Ask yourself, "What about the change made me feel that way?" and "What could I have done to implement the change more quickly or enthusiastically?"
- Complete a personality inventory to identify your strengths and your development needs. Which areas of strength will help you navigate change?

▷▷▷ Prepare for change:

- Consider all the changes you anticipate at work in the next six months. List the benefits you expect from each and the system or process alterations each change will require. Evaluate which aspects of the change you can control or influence.
- Try working in a different physical space, alongside new and different people, or in another department. Changing your surroundings can enable you to see problems from a different perspective and recharge you mentally.
- Invite an expert who is leading a change initiative to a team meeting to describe the purpose and importance of the change. Find out what new skills will be needed and prepare yourself and your team. Ask the expert to outline the benefits to the organization, team, and team members.

▷▷▷ Respond without hesitation:

- When changes are announced, ask leaders in the know to clarify roles, responsibilities, and degree of ownership. Understand that answers to all your questions might not be available right away.
- Don't dwell on the inconvenience or the risk a change brings to you personally. Instead, consider the broader business impact. Ask yourself, "What good could come of this in terms of budget, resources, time, profitability, productivity, morale, customers, or our competition?"
- Choose passion over panic. Find two or three aspects of the change that you believe will lead to big payoffs. Remind yourself (and, if needed, your team) of those things frequently; weigh the pros over the cons.
- Start to rally right away. Think about those the change affects or who needs to implement it and involve them early. Encourage everyone to think creatively about options and give them some say in how to make the change succeed.
- Act with urgency and purpose. Make strides toward the goal every day and identify specific dates for getting things done.

▷▷▷ Learn from those who adapt to change well:

- Develop a network of people throughout your organization who can help you interpret and navigate uncertainty and change. Avoid networks of resistors or naysayers.

- Brainstorm with a colleague the benefits of an upcoming change to your industry, organization, department, team, job, or career. What actions can you take to learn the most from the experience?

- Choose adaptable leaders as role models and observe them during a time of change. Talk with them about what makes them so adaptable. Were they always this way? If not, how did they develop the skills that make them successful? Identify behaviors you could use.

- Read about leaders who successfully adapted to major structural or organizational changes.

▷▷▷ Seek opportunities to immerse yourself in or manage change:

- Volunteer for a task force overseeing a change initiative. To counteract the discomfort and stress of trying something new, take on a responsibility that will leverage one of your strengths.

- Gain confidence in unstructured, unpredictable situations. For example, participate on an innovative project with no precedent or boundaries. Find opportunities to create new processes, work with new people, or come up with new ideas.

- Volunteer for a community project involving a change initiative or an environment with constantly changing variables.

 ## Maximize your **Personal Effectiveness**

Are you already adaptable? Consider these options for applying and further developing your skills:

Lead an investigation or experiment—Because you're likely curious and open to new and different options, you'd be an asset to a team charged with brainstorming and innovation. Use your willingness to seek new information and alternatives—without bias—to find paradigm-shifting approaches that can benefit your organization. Investigate products or services that others might dismiss as too bold or risky. Research new policies or procedures that could boost efficiency.

Tackle an organizational transition—Most organizations—or even teams and departments—experience significant transitions during which structure and strategies change dramatically. People feel uncomfortable in such a stressful environment. Leverage your ability to advocate for change and help others see the benefits. Talk with your manager about how to expand your responsibilities. Ask to take a more prominent role in the next big organizational change.

Continuous Learning

Actively identifying new areas for learning; creating and taking advantage of learning opportunities; using newly gained knowledge and skill on the job.

The Spirit of This Competency

This competency is about demonstrating a passion for learning—creating and making the most of your opportunities to build new knowledge, skills, and experience. It's not learning for learning's sake, but rather its focus is on purposeful, directed learning aimed at solving your pressing business issues. With a strong learning orientation, you maintain your commitment to personal growth in the face of competing priorities and pressure to maintain the status quo. You embrace opportunities to explore possibilities and learn—and not just from your successes; you turn failures into equally important learning opportunities.

 Key Actions: Building Blocks for Success

Key Actions are behaviors that work together to help you demonstrate this competency effectively.

Target learning needs—Identify appropriate areas for learning.

Seek learning opportunities—Identify and participate in learning activities that help fulfill learning needs.

Maximize learning—Actively participate in learning activities in a way that makes the most of the experience (e.g., take notes, ask questions, keep on-the-job application in mind).

Apply knowledge or skill—Put new knowledge, understanding, or skill to practical use on the job; further learning through practice and feedback.

Take risks in learning—Put yourself in unfamiliar or uncomfortable situations in order to learn.

Continuous Learning Can Boost Other Skills

Like other Personal Effectiveness competencies, Continuous Learning skills can be extremely beneficial. They help you to build the knowledge and capabilities needed to address key leadership challenges. Continuous Learning can support your development and enhance your performance in competencies such as:

- Building Partnerships
- Business Acumen
- Coaching
- Creating an Inclusive Environment
- Decision Making
- Driving Innovation
- Facilitating Change

How strong is your learning orientation?

If you embrace learning, you:

- Realize that personal growth is a continuous process, not an event.
- Look at both failures and successes in a productive way—as opportunities to learn.
- Request feedback from others by asking what you can do or learn to be more effective.
- Suspend judgment on new ideas. First you ask questions to understand and then you pose challenges.
- View colleagues as valuable sources of information and partners in learning (and not as barriers).
- Look for data, insights, and experiences from multiple, diverse sources.
- Share what you've learned and encourage others to do the same.

Could you improve your learning orientation?

If you hesitate to build your skills or improve your knowledge, your tendencies and behaviors could be getting in the way of your success.

Taking the time to learn can interfere with other priorities, and some people are content with their current knowledge and skills. With markets, products, and technology evolving at such a fast pace, however, even a slight tendency to resist learning something new can affect your success. Which of your tendencies help you? Which get in the way of your desired results, and what can you do to improve?

Effective Behaviors	Troublesome Tendencies	Temper Your Tendencies
Do you:	Instead, do you:	Try this:
Look for opportunities to learn something new?	• Delegate tasks that you don't have the knowledge or skills to execute? • Assume you know all you need to be effective in your role? • Avoid attending seminars, conferences, etc.? • Prefer status-quo approaches? • Learn the minimum necessary to meet requirements? • Avoid reflecting on failed efforts?	• Realize that growth in learning is a continuous process. Find impromptu opportunities to learn (e.g., use search engines for quick research and talk with your colleagues about unfamiliar topics). • Stay abreast of organizational changes and expectations so you know what knowledge and skills you'll need. Locate (ask your manager or HR department for help) both formal and informal learning opportunities. • Use a variety of settings and modalities that appeal to different learning styles. • Request feedback about what you can do or learn to be more effective.
Actively participate in learning?	• Multitask during workshops, webinars, etc.? • Avoid taking notes? • Assume what you're learning is irrelevant to you or your team? • Hesitate to participate in follow-up activities and skill practices?	• Remove electronic devices or other distractors from your learning environment. • Ask questions about what you're learning and talk with others about real-world applications. Ask for an explanation when a concept is unclear. Summarize what you've learned to check your understanding. • While practice or knowledge checks might seem unnecessary, they can help you—especially if you can't apply what you learned right away.
Apply what you learn?	• Struggle to bring new ideas and techniques into your work? • Quickly lose enthusiasm for what you learn? • Stick with old ways of thinking? • Avoid asking for feedback on how you're applying new skills?	• Look for ways to apply new learning, despite organizational constraints (e.g., outdated policies, lack of resources). Advocate for best practices and creative solutions. • Talk to your colleagues about your learning experience (e.g., describe what was interesting or confusing). Encourage them to share their experiences. • Invite your manager, peers, and team to give you feedback on how effectively you're integrating new knowledge and skills.

16

Effective Behaviors	Troublesome Tendencies	Temper Your Tendencies
Do you:	Instead, do you:	Try this:
Take risks in learning?	• Prefer to learn in safe, familiar environments? • Focus learning on what will have an immediate payoff? • Worry that you might fail if you try something new? • Hesitate to apply new knowledge and skills in a high-profile assignment?	• Try a setting or modality that pushes you out of your comfort zone. Consider using more (or less) technology. • Learn something simply because you're interested in it, not because your work requires it. You might use it in ways you don't expect. • Ask your manager for extra support—even assign a mentor—on new or high-visibility projects. • Mentally redefine a mistake as an opportunity to learn.

Development Activities

Developing Personal Effectiveness competencies is a balance of counteracting detrimental tendencies with constructive behavior. The following development activities for Continuous Learning can guide improvements in your self-awareness, skills, and behavior. They also can be part of your longer-term development plan.

▷▷▷ Assess your learning needs:

- Think of times you resisted learning something new. What were the circumstances? Why did you resist? Reflect on your emotional reactions and then try to identify and address whatever was getting in your way.

- Ask for feedback from your manager, peers, direct reports or even customers about what skills are strong and what you can improve. Keep an open mind and then decide where to focus your development. Set a SMART goal for what you'll learn, how you'll learn it, and by when. Ensure that it is specific and measurable, has accountability for results, and is relevant and time bound.

- Complete a learning styles inventory to determine how you learn best. Which delivery methods hold your attention and help you retain what you learned? Do you prefer to learn independently, or are you more motivated in a group? Do you learn best by observing others or jumping in and trying it yourself? Find the strategies that work best for you.

- Consider what will be new or different about your work in six months to a year. What will you or your team need to learn to be prepared? Start a defined learning journey right away. Learning new knowledge and skills under pressure and with little time to practice can be stressful.

16

▷▷▷ Make learning and personal growth part of your regular activities:

- Keep a list of skills you'd like to learn. Set aside a day or a few hours every month to take part in learning activities. Keep a file of the information and tools you gain. Periodically review these materials and look for new ways to use them.

- Attend conferences and networking events regularly and stay in touch with your contacts. They might lead to interesting opportunities beyond your work or organization.

- Use less-than-successful outcomes as learning opportunities. Hold "post-mortems" after each project to review what went well and what could be done better the next time. Where would a new approach have been better than a tried-and-true solution? If knowledge or skills gaps interfered with success, create a plan to address those gaps before the next project.

▷▷▷ Seek opportunities to learn new things:

- Partner with your organization's learning allies. Human Resources can give you advice and resources for enhancing your skills. Ask them to recommend experiences that will increase your knowledge of other business areas.

- Stimulate different parts of your brain by focusing on something other than your daily routine. For example, if you work on a computer most days, look for opportunities to work with your hands or to be screen-free. Similarly, if your work includes regimented processes, look for activities that encourage creativity.

- Set up your media feeds so that you get daily or weekly reminders about the latest technical, market, and industry information. To get the most impact, prioritize content relevance over entertainment value, and unfollow anyone who isn't sharing clear, relatable, and current information.

- When volunteering for task force assignments or other projects, push yourself to take on new roles that take you out of your comfort zone and force you to experiment with new skills and knowledge.

- Create learning tension—that is, the motivation and urgency to learn. Learning tension builds when you are challenged to show what you can do within a specific time frame to address a real work situation. Your manager can help you formalize your learning goals into a performance or development plan with tight—but realistic—time frames.

16

▷▷▷ Be a positive model for learning:

- Force yourself to be a learner and show your vulnerabilities. By doing so, you make it safe for others to take risks. If they encounter obstacles or feel uncertain, they can take comfort in knowing you faced the same challenges.

- Develop a list of valuable learning resources and build a library of tools and materials (books, articles, websites, tips, tools, best practices, and social media tools). Share them with your colleagues. Don't hoard information under the misguided notion that "knowledge is power."

- Assign each team member responsibility for learning about a key topic (e.g., technologies, processes, or procedures). One person could be an expert on competitors, while another masters a challenging software. Match the assignments to people's interests and career aspirations but rotate them periodically so that people explore a variety of topics.

- Be an advocate for experimentation. Create low-risk projects or teams where people can try new things. Even if an experiment fails, reward and recognize those bold enough to take chances.

- Don't let key people leave your team without encouraging them to pass on their knowledge and insights to others. Always be looking to build the next generation of experts.

Maximize your **Personal Effectiveness**

Do you already have a strong learning orientation? Consider these options for applying and further developing your skills:

Lead a reading group—Once a quarter, gather people—perhaps over lunch—who have similar interests and discuss a recent study, article, video, webinar, podcast, or blog. Ask everyone to review the content in advance Encourage them to share their reactions. What was most interesting, surprising, or valuable? What can you apply in your organization or team?

Be the subject matter expert (SME)—Identify a topic, skill, or technology that you know well (or want to know well) or work closely with a vendor to become an expert on their equipment, product, or service. Learn all you can about the subject and commit to keep learning. Be the go-to, "nobody knows it better" person. Formalize your learning with a certification, if available, and volunteer to train others.

Driving for Results

Setting high goals for personal and group accomplishment; working tenaciously to achieve objectives; using measurement methods to monitor progress.

The Spirit of This Competency

This competency is about striving for excellence—being both a strong starter and finisher. To be a results-oriented leader, you set challenging goals that bring out the best in yourself and others. You have a personal accountability that drives you to make meaningful contributions to your organization. You aren't easily distracted or deterred. Instead, you anticipate and overcome obstacles. You're adept at finding ways to manage time, persist, and renew your personal energy so you can achieve critical long-term objectives.

 Key Actions: Building Blocks for Success

Key Actions are behaviors that work together to help you demonstrate this competency effectively.

Target opportunities—Systematically evaluate business opportunities, targeting those with the greatest potential for producing positive results.

Establish stretch goals—Set challenging goals for yourself and others.

Achieve goals—Work tenaciously to overcome obstacles and to meet or exceed goals.

Stay focused—Remain self-disciplined; measure progress and evaluate results; reprioritize as appropriate; prevent irrelevant issues or distractions from interfering with completing tasks on time.

16

Driving for Results can boost other skills

Like other Personal Effectiveness competencies, Driving for Results can help you to build the knowledge and capabilities needed to address key leadership challenges, especially those requiring focus, persistence, and discipline. Driving for Results can support your development and enhance your performance in competencies such as:

- Building Partnerships
- Business Acumen
- Coaching
- Decision Making
- Delegation and Empowerment
- Driving Innovation
- Facilitating Change
- Guiding Team Success
- Influencing

How effectively do you drive results?

If you work tenaciously toward achievement and improved performance, you:

- Regularly set and reach challenging goals working with your team.
- Make visible and considerable contributions to your work group and the organization. Others can readily describe your and your team's efforts, passion, and accomplishments.
- Ensure your team's work is energetic and purposeful. They don't waste time "spinning their wheels" on shifting priorities or low-value projects.
- Are clear about who is accountable for specific outcomes and frequently ask for progress updates.
- Aren't daunted by obstacles or delayed by distractions. Setbacks are infrequent and resolved quickly.

Could you improve your results orientation?

If you hesitate to set and energetically work toward challenging goals, your tendencies and behaviors could be getting in the way of your success.

It can be difficult to stay committed to a project or goal when you have many demands on your time. You might avoid taking on anything that appears to be too challenging. Or, if you do get started, you might abandon the work if obstacles seem insurmountable or distractions continually interfere with your progress. Which of your tendencies help you? Which get in the way of your desired results, and what can you do to improve?

Effective Behaviors	Troublesome Tendencies	Temper Your Tendencies
Do you:	**Instead, do you:**	**Try this:**
Identify oppor-tunities that will have the greatest business impact?	• Spend time on things that produce limited benefits? • Find comfort in the status quo? • Overlook long-term business objectives in favor of personal or team needs? • Get involved in too many things? • Create a sense of urgency on every initiative?	• Focus on initiatives that have the greatest potential for meaningful re-sults, using criteria to evaluate them. Get guidance from key stakeholders and consider the broader organiza-tion's goals and values. • Is juggling too many projects causing you to lose focus and energy? Assign each project a different priority. Give one or two major projects your full attention, so you can remain effective. • Make sure your team members know their priorities too. Don't create an unwarranted sense of urgency or de-mand perfection on every project.
Set challenging goals?	• Prefer quick and easy assignments? • Take on projects where your current skills are enough? • Fear your team will resist working any harder? • Take the path of least resistance? • Wait for your man-ager to give you new assignments?	• It can be tempting to keep things simple or make incremental improve-ments, but are you making an impact? An easy goal will fail to provide a real sense of accomplishment. • Find opportunities for you or your team to shine. Volunteer for a project with high stakes. Be the team to say, "We'll do it!" when others hesitate. • Be ready for more than your current role or skill set. Ask your manager how your role might evolve and work to develop next-level capabilities. Do the same with your team.
Work to overcome obstacles and avoid distractions?	• Abandon a project at the first sign of trouble? • Procrastinate or quickly lose interest in assignments? • Try to please everyone? • Get easily distracted by the next big thing? • Have a ready explanation for why you haven't met your goals?	• Don't let setbacks paralyze you. Come up with creative solutions that will enable you to see the work through. • Reinvigorate waning efforts by bring-ing in an extra resource or a fresh point of view. Meet with a stakeholder to be reminded of the project's pur-pose and importance. • Realize the difference between moti-vating a "stuck" team and pressuring people to perform. Provide encour-agement and positive reinforcement. • Don't mistake being busy for being productive. Create project plans with defined milestones. If there isn't progress, find out why. Work with your manager and other groups (HR, Finance, etc.) to remove barriers.

16

Effective Behaviors	Troublesome Tendencies	Temper Your Tendencies
Do you:	**Instead, do you:**	**Try this:**
Ensure accountability	• Assume people understand your expectations? • Notice that your team is confused about roles or performance expectations? • Miss deadlines so frequently that it's almost expected?	• Make sure people understand what they are accountable for doing and by when. • Consider a mistake as an opportunity to learn, not a reason to pull someone from a project or key role. Provide coaching right away if someone lacks accountability or capability. • Don't let missed deadlines become your modus operandi. If your or your team's expectations are too ambitious, negotiate with your manager or stakeholders for more realistic goals. • Keep everyone's goals SMART—specific, measurable, achievable, relevant, and time bound. • Check in periodically with each person. Don't assume information provided at kickoff will be remembered or stay relevant.
Track and measure results?	• Dread having to report on progress or show quantifiable results? • Feel surprised that you aren't making better progress? • Miss opportunities to show your team the results of their efforts?	• Try a setting or modality that pushes you out of your comfort zone. Consider using more (or less) technology. • Learn something simply because you're interested in it, not because your work requires it. You might use it in ways you don't expect. • Ask your manager for extra support—even assign a mentor—on new or high-visibility projects. • Mentally redefine a mistake as an opportunity to learn.

16

Development Activities

Developing Personal Effectiveness competencies is a balance of counter-acting detrimental tendencies with constructive behavior. The following development activities for Driving for Results can guide improvements in your self-awareness, skills, and behavior. They also can be part of your longer-term development plan.

▷▷▷ Evaluate how well your and your team's activities link to important business outcomes:

- Were the achievements of the past few months more task- or team-oriented as opposed to strategically focused? Will the results have a short- or long-term effect? Does the organization or the team benefit more? Work with your manager to find projects that will have further-reaching impact.

- List your daily activities, and where you allocate your time. Which activities have a positive impact on business results? Create a "stop doing" list for any activities that don't have bottom-line impact and a "delegate" list for those that aren't the best use of your time and skills.

- Are you working on projects that might not get done on time? Are projects competing for the same resources or funding? Run an impact/effort analysis (i.e., time invested versus value added) to prioritize the one that will yield the maximum bottom-line results.

- Get your team's thoughts on priorities and workload. Ask each person: Is it clear what you should be working on? Do you have the time and resources to be successful? What three things can we do stop doing to help you get better results?

- Ask your team, manager, and peers for feedback on your time management. Would they say you procrastinate? Do you cause delays that affect others? Do you avoid some types of tasks? Evaluate your motivations and choices and examine the consequences.

▷▷▷ Create an environment that encourages striving for success:

- Share financial and competitive information with your team and let them know how their contributions directly and indirectly affect those outcomes. Encourage team members to get involved in projects where their unique skills and interests would help get things done faster and better.

- Encourage your team members to act on objectives and goals or to take ownership of an improvement initiative without waiting for you to delegate or give direction. You do the same—don't expect your manager to suggest or approve every action.

- Demonstrate your enthusiasm for and commitment to projects. Present a can-do attitude, approaching challenges with optimism and vigor.

16

- Recognize staff members who volunteer for difficult or undesirable projects but don't expect the "usual suspects" to take on the most challenging assignments every time. Otherwise, they'll quickly get frustrated and overwhelmed. Encourage everyone to try new things and build team capability; that way, if one resource isn't available, another is ready.

▷▷▷ Maintain momentum and make progress:

- During a project's start-up phase, brainstorm potential obstacles and problems as a team and develop contingency plans. If a project seems to be failing, look at alternatives that might lead to success, eliminate obstacles, make necessary changes, or start over.

- To keep progress toward goals on track, establish milestones, check-in times, and due dates. Frequently communicate progress with your team (but not so frequently that a slight dip in performance becomes a premature concern).

- Use project management tools and software. Look for ones that have built-in reminders and methods to share regular team updates.

- Learn to say no or at least to offer alternatives to stakeholders. It's usually not feasible to agree to every request. Don't let your desire to appeal to stakeholders jeopardize your team's morale or results. Work with the requester to brainstorm alternatives. Ask: Who else might do the work? What could be completed sooner and what later?

- As a project or task is completed, start working on the next project. Don't let formal authorizations slow you down if you feel confident getting started on what's coming next.

▷▷▷ Set and achieve ambitious goals:

- When your team receives a new project that has defined expectations and outputs, ask, "How can we do even better?" Get their ideas on what additional (yet achievable) goals would challenge them or impress and inform stakeholders about their talent and potential.

Maximize your **Personal Effectiveness**

Are you already very results oriented? Consider these options for applying and further developing your skills:

Take charge of a struggling project—If you see a team grappling to make progress or running into frequent barriers, volunteer to take a leadership role or to act as an unbiased auditor. What are their challenges? What advice can you offer? Maintain the team's confidence and esteem by making it clear that you're an advisor, not a fixer. Disclose your own lessons learned and look for opportunities to coach the team's leaders. Use your experience to identify any obstacles or inefficient processes. Offer your knowledge and network to help them overcome barriers.

Find a "stretch" project for your team—Review longer-term organizational goals to find a more strategically oriented project for your team (i.e., one that allows your team to affect the organization's economic viability, longevity, or competitive position). It might seem daunting at first, but rally your team to try something bold. Find out what people need (tools, skills) and set individual performance goals. Hold everyone accountable; don't be too forgiving—differentiate excuses from true barriers. Prioritize the new project. Secure a senior leader to be your team's champion; create visibility for the team's work and celebrate their success.

16